*Group Thinking
and Conference
Leadership*

William E. Utterback
THE OHIO STATE UNIVERSITY

Group Thinking and Conference Leadership

REVISED EDITION

HOLT, RINEHART and WINSTON, Inc.
New York · Chicago · San Francisco
Toronto · London

Preface
to the
Revised Edition

The present edition, like the first, is a practical treatise. It includes only such theory as seems likely to deepen insight, mature judgment, or sharpen skill in discussion. To achieve this purpose more effectively I have in both text and Appendix included new material. Pattern in discussion, for example, is discussed more fully than in the first edition, and in connection with participation attention is given to the variety of functions the participant may usefully perform as well as to the roles he should avoid; and such special devices as role-playing and the "buzz" session are considered. Perhaps the principal additions are the inclusion in the Appendix of seventy-one case problems as material for practice, with suggestions to the student on their use, and two new radio panel discussions on subjects of current interest. While the book still contains advice for those interested primarily in discussing controversial public questions, inclusion of the problems reflects my conviction that such problems, for at least a considerable part of the course in discussion, are more effective than public questions in developing judgment and skill at the conference table. The *Instructor's Manual,* which accompanies the book, contains suggestions for the use both of the case problems and of public questions as the subject matter of practice sessions.

In addition to the acknowledgments made in the preface to the first edition I wish to express my appreciation of the help received from other colleagues more recently associated with me in teaching courses in discussion at The Ohio State University, especially to Arthur Angrist, Lester Breniman, Keith Brooks, James Dee, Herbert Goyer, Algrid Grybas, Harold F. Harding, Ruth B. Lewis, John T. Rickey, Raymond Ross, and Eugene Vasilew.

W.E.U.

January, 1964

Preface
to the
First Edition

This book is concerned with cooperative thinking as a democratic procedure. It is addressed to those who serve on committees, boards, and councils; to those who attend staff meetings and conferences; to those who talk over common problems in community organizations or in the church, school, or office—to all, in short, who participate in or lead informal discussion in small groups or who are preparing to do so. Its purpose is a practical one—to promote more effective group thinking.

In order to provide detailed practical advice rather than a comprehensive theoretical treatise, I have ignored such forms of discussion as the forum, the symposium, and the debate, which are adequately dealt with elsewhere, and have devoted the entire volume to a detailed consideration of one form—informal discussion in the small group. The methods recommended here have grown out of practical experience and have been tested repeatedly in leading discussion, in conducting training institutes for discussion leaders, and in teaching courses in discussion methods.

The book is organized in three major sections. The first presents those general principles applicable to all discussion involving group thinking. The second considers some of the logical and psychological aspects of thinking, with special reference to the tasks of preparing for and participating in discussion. The third deals with the special problems encountered in several typical discussion situations. The Appendix includes material for use in the classroom, suggestions regarding the organization of courses in discussion, and two radio panel discussions which demonstrate principles and techniques analyzed in the text.

While the short illustrative passages scattered through the body of the text are based on actual discussions, the names and places mentioned are in every case fictitious. The two radio panel discussions included in the Appendix, however, were presented at the time and place and by the persons mentioned in the introductory paragraphs.

It is impossible to acknowledge adequately my debt to previous writers on group discussion. Those I have found especially helpful are mentioned frequently in the short bibliographies appended to the chapters. Nor can I estimate the even greater debt I owe to the groups I have led in discussion, the discussion leaders with whom I have conferred, and the students with whom I have worked in the classroom. All have contributed much to the following pages.

More specific acknowledgment of assistance is due those associated with me in the teaching of discussion courses at The Ohio State University: Mortimer L. Feigenbaum, Wallace C. Fotheringham, Mary W. Graham, James A. Grissinger, and Mary E. Ludlum. Finally, for editorial assistance in preparing the manuscript I am heavily indebted to my wife, Helen Tappan Utterback.

WILLIAM E. UTTERBACK

Columbus, Ohio
December, 1949

Contents

*Group Thinking
and Conference
Leadership*

CHAPTER 1

Decision through Discussion

The conference table is rapidly becoming an indispensable tool of modern civilization. Conference is democracy at work, and the chief problems which threaten our society admit of no solution except through the democratic process. Essentially these problems are: How can large numbers of people cooperate without surrendering their freedom to a dictator? How can they settle their conflicts without resorting to violence? Neither problem is soluble except at the conference table. Consequently, each year more of the world's business is conducted by small groups seated around tables attempting to reach collective decisions through cooperative discussion.

What Is Group Discussion?

We may observe the use of informal discussion as a social tool in almost any area of social life and at any level of cooperative action from the simplest committee meeting to a conference of foreign ministers. Let us look in on the world at work.

In a typical American town the program committee of a businessmen's luncheon club is in session:

Mr. Brown: I think we've overdone entertainment. Our members have had enough of parlor magic and funny stories.

Chairman: You want speeches on political topics?

Mr. Brown: Why not?

Mr. Caldwell: We had something of the sort last fall. The talks were pretty dull.

Mr. Clayman: The problem is to find really good speakers on live topics. It's hard to do in a town of this size. But there are several possibilities. . . .

Meanwhile down the street in the office of a business firm department heads are seated around a table:

Sales Manager: I tell you the day of coal as a household fuel is on the way out, at least in this area. Gas is cleaner, and the idea is catching on. We have inquiries every day about converting to gas.

Production Manager: But the supply of gas is too uncertain in Ohio. Remember the trouble gas users had last winter!

Treasurer: It seems to me the problem is whether we should take a long- or a short-range view. If we start installing gas furnaces now, we won't pick up much business in that line for a few years. But the present gas shortage is only a transportation problem. It won't last.

President: Right! But apart from the temporary gas shortage, is the trend really toward the use of gas? Have you any figures on that, Keegan? . . .

In another office of the same firm a committee tackles a shop problem:

Mr. Sorensen: The problem, as I see it, is this—On the third floor every machine operator loses time waiting for a dolly to bring material to his machine.

Foreman Cummings: There are ten dollies on the floor. What more do you want?

Mr. Talladay: The trouble is—when material is brought to a machine, it isn't unloaded. The operator unloads it as he uses the material.

Mr. Carlson: And that makes a good deal of sense. To unload the material and then pick it up from the floor is a waste of time.

Mr. Sorensen: Just the same, half the dollies are tied up most of the time.

Chairman: Do you know, Cummings, whether all of the dollies on the other floors are in use? . . .

Not many blocks away a council made up of ten representative citizens is considering a community problem:

Mr. Holmes: The teen-agers are the heart of the problem. That's my observation, and the report from the police department bears it out.

Chairman: Our playground facilities are fairly adequate now, aren't they?

Father Kelley: I would say, yes. That situation has been improved a good deal.

Mr. Cane: But this isn't a playground problem. The trouble occurs in the evening. The youngsters have nothing to do but roam the streets. We are doing what we can for the boys in the YM and through the Scout Council, but it isn't enough.

Mrs. Cohen: It seems to me what we need is some kind of social center that can be kept open under proper supervision from seven to ten in the evening. . . .

While the community council explores the problem of a social center, classes are in session at the high school. The class in social studies has just viewed a short film entitled "Democracy":

Teacher: According to the film, we don't have democracy if power is concentrated in a few hands while a majority of the people have nothing to say about how government is run. Using this definition as a yardstick, would you say that student activities here are run democratically?

John: Not by a long shot! There are five on the student council, and they run the whole show.

Helen: Not entirely. Sometimes they put things to a vote during an assembly period.

Edward: But not very often; most of the time they settle it.

Carol: Suppose they do. How else can you get anything done? Besides, everybody gets to vote when the council is elected.

Edward: But how many vote? Very few.

Helen: Whose fault is that? Everyone can vote if he likes. What more can you ask?

Edward: Well, it's the fault of the students, then, not the fault of the system. Just the same, democracy isn't working right if only a few vote. . . .

And that evening at the home of Mr. Hanson fifteen friends and neighbors are seated in a circle in the living room:

Moderator: In our discussion of the European Common Market we come now to the question: Is the Common Market a good thing for its present members? What do you think?

Mrs. Tyler: I certainly think it is. They are lowering tariffs against each other to permit a free flow of goods. This means that industries in each country have a profitable international market in Europe.

Mr. Faucet: But doesn't it mean, too, that those industries in each country that do not have a natural advantage will be put out of business by competitors in other countries?

Dr. Catlan: Quite true. But this will be only temporary. When the capital and labor now involved in such industries have transferred to a line of business where they do have a natural advantage, everyone will be better off. Consumers will benefit in all countries.

Mrs. Tyler: Yes, and this is already beginning to happen. All countries participating in the Common Market are on the way up economically.

Various as are the subjects and situations, these samples of discussion have much in common. In each the group is small, usually between five and twenty. No speeches are being delivered. Discussion is taking the form of informal conversation in which all participate freely and equally. In each group a leader is directing conversation to a specific problem or topic.

This is group discussion as we shall understand it in the pages to follow. We may distinguish it from casual social conversation, which is undirected and seldom sticks long to one topic. We may distinguish it from various forms of public discussion: from public address, in which a few speak while an audience listens; from a forum, in which many may speak from the floor but in which discussion takes the form of short talks rather than of informal conversation; and from the question period following a public address, in which members of the audience address questions to the speaker. These forms of discussion are all useful in their time and place, but our concern will be with informal discussion in the small group.

Why Discussion?

The values of such discussion are partly practical, partly educational.

In committee, staff meeting, labor-management conference, or community council the practical advantages of decision by cooperative discussion arise from the nature of the administrative process. To be successful a policy must be soundly conceived and must receive the wholehearted support of those who are to execute it. In formulating the policy the more wealth of information, suggestion, and viewpoint that can be brought to bear, the better. It is seldom that one person, however well informed, can match the resources of a group whose members bring a varied background to discussion of a problem. In planning a community recreational program, for example, the scout master, the YMCA director, the heads of social agencies, the business and religious leaders, the teacher, the parent—all have something to contribute. A new policy hammered out in discussion by all of those who have something to contribute is likely to be sounder than a policy formulated by one person alone.

And when those who are to execute the policy have had a hand in its making, they put more intelligence and energy into its execution. If discussion is continued until substantial agreement is reached, the thinking of each member is represented in the conclusion. Each feels that the decision is in part his own, and execution of the policy is not embarrassed by apathy or hostility of a disgruntled minority.

These practical advantages of group thinking are compelling reasons for making cooperative discussion part of the administrative process. But discussion has educational values as well, perhaps best illustrated by a community round-table discussion devoted to consideration of a political or economic problem on which the group will not take collective action. Here the object is to help each member make up his own mind on the question, and it matters little whether agreement is reached. The individual participant benefits in several ways.

In the first place, few experiences so effectively develop a lively and continuing interest in a public problem as does earnest, thoughtful discussion in a small group. What we do something about becomes interesting and important to us. And earnestly to discuss, say, the Berlin question is to do at least something about it. The member of a round table is not a passive spectator. He states his own view, hears it criticized, returns to its defense, perhaps modifying it as he does so. The more he handles the problem in discussion, the more real it becomes to him. It is a common observation that at the close of discussion members seldom leave the room immediately. They stand around in knots of two or three still discussing the problem, and usually they may still be heard in earnest conversation as they go up the street. They have developed an interest in the question that will prompt them to read further on it, to listen to speeches or television programs dealing with it, and to discuss it with their friends. It is difficult to overestimate the quickening of interest in public affairs that results from regular participation in discussion of this kind.

The participant finds himself progressively better informed on public questions. Discussion whets his appetite for more serious and purposeful reading than he would be likely to do otherwise. And the information brought out in the course of discussion adds to his knowledge. The question here is not by what method most information can be laid before a group, but rather by what method a group can be brought to assimilate and make practical use of most information. Reading a book or listening to a speech is usually a passive process, and most of what goes in one ear, or eye, soon goes out the other. But when we put information to practical use in discussion, we do not soon forget it.

Discussion clarifies, as well as enriches, the participant's thinking. The confusion or error in one's thinking about a public question is peculiar to himself. It can seldom be removed by a public speaker, who cannot address himself to the individual but must deliver a broadside of information and argument at the audience as a whole. In discussion one must state and defend his views. If he is in error, the group will set him right. If he is confused, the necessity he is under of stating his views will force him to think more clearly.

In addition to quickening one's interest in public affairs and enriching and clarifying one's thinking about them, discussion develops two attitudes highly desirable in themselves. One is the attitude of objectivity toward ideas and arguments, a virtue as rare as it is basic to straight thinking. When Smith and Brown disagree, Smith is likely to think of Brown's argument as a weapon with which Brown is trying to strike him. He is likely also to think of his own argument as a weapon to use against Brown. Only with difficulty do we bring ourselves to dissociate an idea or an argument from personality and to regard it as an object of interest in its own right which we can handle and examine disinterestedly as we might examine a physical object. There is no better place to learn this difficult lesson than in the discussion group, where the consequences of emotional and wishful thinking are so immediately obvious.

Finally, the discipline of thinking together does much to develop a sympathetic attitude toward those who disagree with us. In discussion we cannot simply shout the other fellow down; if we are to reach agreement, we must listen to what he is saying and make the effort necessary to understand him. It usually turns out that there is at least something in what he is saying. And when he realizes that we understand his point and appreciate its value, that we are trying to incorporate it into the larger pattern of growing truth which the group is working out together, he becomes more willing to examine our argument sympathetically. With experience in discussion we come to feel that almost anything another believes earnestly probably has at least a grain of truth in it, however deeply it may be buried in error or confusion. To act on this assumption habitually is to be truly liberal.

Discussion and the Democratic Process

The practical and educational values of group discussion are of concern to the groups and individuals immediately involved. Looking at the matter more broadly, one may observe also that discussion is an essential part of the democratic process.

Democracy has been defined as government by talk. Though a partial definition, the statement comes near to the truth. In any organized society people must work together—voluntarily, as in a democracy, or under coercion, as in an autocracy. People will seldom cooperate voluntarily in either committee or nation except as action is based on collective decision reached through cooperative thinking. And to think together we must talk together. From the simplest neighborhood organization to the United Nations, therefore, government is conducted in large part by conference.

We take it for granted that conferences will be the order of the day in government at higher levels—in executive offices and in legislative committee rooms. We do not always appreciate the necessity for conferences at the grass-roots level. But here also, and here especially, democracy flourishes or withers according as there is much or little public interest finding expression in earnest, thoughtful, and informed discussion. The more such discussion we have, the better—in the church, in the school, in the labor union and in the managerial office, in community organizations, and at the neighborhood round table.

But we must be concerned with the quality as well as with the quantity of discussion. As many members of committees or round tables can testify, much group discussion is too ill-informed and poorly conducted to serve any purpose. The quality of democracy at all levels needs to be improved by more and better discussion. We must disabuse ourselves of the comfortable illusion that discussion, like breathing and walking, is something that anyone can do well without thought, effort, or knowledge of method. In the following pages attention will be pinpointed on processes of making group thinking more profitable, whether in the cooperative solution of practical problems, as in the committee or staff meeting, or in the enrichment and clarification of individual thinking, as in the schoolroom or at the community round table.

References

Braden, Waldo W. and Earnest Brandenburg, *Oral Decision-Making*, New York: Harper & Row, Publishers, 1955, Chap. 1.

Ferguson, Charles W., *A Little Democracy Is a Dangerous Thing*, New York: Association Press, 1948.

Gulley, Halbert E., *Discussion, Conference, and Group Process*, New York: Holt, Rinehart and Winston, Inc., 1960, Chaps. 1, 2.

Lasker, Bruno, *Democracy Through Discussion*, New York: H. W. Wilson Co., 1949, Chaps. 1, 2.

PART ONE

TECHNIQUES
OF DISCUSSION

CHAPTER 2

When Is Discussion Profitable?

It must not be supposed that the conference table possesses the magic property of generating wisdom when rubbed simultaneously by a dozen pairs of elbows. As we shall observe in future chapters, success depends on the skill brought to the table by moderator and participants. It depends also on the physical arrangements that have been made in advance of the meeting, on the make-up and attitude of the group itself, on the question selected for discussion, and on the leader's provisions for making information available to the group. Without the conditions necessary for effective group thinking, the moderator can do little to make discussion profitable.

Setting the Stage

Satisfactory physical arrangements are more important than might be supposed. This is true especially of the seating arrangement. Members of the group should be seated close together; they have more feeling of belonging to the group when they touch elbows. And they should be able to see each other and the moderator without turning around. Good discussion is almost impossible when the group is seated primly in rows, as in an auditorium, or when it is scattered about in a large room.

Probably the best arrangement is to seat members around a large table. If a number of small tables are available, they may be arranged in a hollow square with members seated around the outside facing each other. They should not be set end to end, making one long narrow table, as is often done in hotel conference rooms; members seated on the same side of the table cannot see each other.

Frequently no table of any kind is available, as when a group meets in the living room of a private home. In this case members should sit in a semicircle facing the leader. For a larger group chairs are arranged in a double semicircle.

A portable blackboard placed where all can see it and where the leader can turn to it conveniently will be found useful. And wall space for the display of diagrams, charts, and maps is desirable.

Discussion is necessarily a leisurely process, and adequate time for it must be available. It is a mistake to schedule a conference at an hour when discussion must be hurried or many of the members must leave early. It is equally unwise to protract discussion to the point of fatigue. A single session should seldom last longer than two hours, and for many groups an hour and a half is better. If a conference is to remain in session throughout the day, a brief recess every hour and a half will improve the quality of discussion.

The Group

In organizing a committee, conference, or discussion group one must recognize that success depends a good deal on the constitution of the group itself and on the conception of discussion its members bring to the meeting.

Fruitful discussion is impossible in a group too large for informal conversation. Most experienced discussion leaders agree that twenty are about as many as can participate profitably. A larger group soon divides into the few who talk and the many who listen. If discussion is to be attempted with a larger group, certain adaptations of the method (to be discussed in Chapter 9) may be employed. On the other hand, as few as three or four may discuss a problem profitably if the members represent a sufficient diversity of background and viewpoint.

The group should be composed of persons genuinely interested in the problem to be discussed. Very few can enjoy or contribute much to discussion of what they consider an academic topic. When membership is fixed, as in clubs or neighborhood round tables that meet regularly, the problem is one of selecting topics to fit group interests. We shall say more of this presently. But when a committee is being appointed or a conference is being organized to consider a given problem, care should be taken to include on the committee or to invite to the conference those who are vitally concerned with the problem—those whose personal or community interests are involved, those who will be expected to cooperate in carrying out any policy adopted.

Given a community of interest in the problem to be discussed, the more diversity of background and viewpoint represented in the group, the better. If a group of neighbors is to discuss a national or international question, the more nearly it represents a cross section of the political views of the community, the more lively and fruitful discussion will be. The tendency of birds of a feather to flock together promotes congeniality, but it does not make for good discussion. The same principle holds for a committee or community council concerned with solution of a practical problem. Persons of contrasting views and backgrounds bring to the conference table the richness of information and suggestion essential to good discussion.

A group of the right size, inspired by common interest in a question, and bringing to a meeting a rich variety of experience, should be capable of profitable discussion.

How fruitful this discussion will be, however, will depend somewhat on group conception of the nature and purpose of discussion. When a group unused to the method is meeting for the first time, it may be worth while to suggest to its members that informal discussion is best thought of as a cooperative problem-solving activity aiming at consensus rather than at decision by a majority vote.

The conception of discussion as a cooperative enterprise implies that all members participate freely and on a basis of equality, no one expecting to be told what to think or to tell others what to think. It implies also that so far as is humanly possible each member holds his opinion tentatively and subject to revision. In discussion we are inquirers, not advocates, and those who are certain they already know all the answers can contribute little.

It is useful, too, to remember that the group is meeting not to talk about a topic, but to attempt the solution of a problem. The problem-solving nature of the business under consideration in a committee or staff meeting is usually too obvious to be missed. But many groups are content to discuss somewhat vaguely such topics as atomic energy, the status of the Negro in American life, or the role of good will in industrial relations. Better discussion will usually result if a specific problem is proposed for discussion and worded interrogatively as a question to which the group will seek an answer: Should atomic energy be placed under international control? Would a federal antipoll-tax law improve the Negro's status in the South? How can good will best be developed in labor-management relations? The problem-solving attitude gives purpose and direction to the thinking of the group.

And the group should try to reach consensus on the question discussed rather than settle its differences by voting. When successful discussion has run its full course, differences of opinion are resolved to the satisfaction of all. At the end of the session no one feels that the truth as he now sees it has been compromised or that he has been overpowered by weight of numbers. In practice this ideal is not always attainable, but to resort too quickly to a vote as a method of settling the many differences of opinion that arise is to miss the spirit and purpose of group discussion.

The Problem

Problems suitable for group discussion are of many kinds, but perhaps most of them could be grouped under three heads: group action, public policy, and personal conduct.

By problems of group action we mean those in which the object is to formulate a policy which the group itself, acting collectively or through a representative, will put into operation or will recommend for action. The community council, the policy-forming committee, the staff, the grievance committee, and local organizations of all kinds engaged in management of their own affairs deal primarily with problems of this type. The problem to be discussed is of immediate and local concern; the end in view is action by the group; and substantial agreement must be reached before the discussion can be considered successful. In situations of this kind there is little opportunity to select a problem with a view to its suitability for discussion. The problem is already at hand, and the group must find a solution if it can.

Problems of public policy are those dealing with community, state, national, or international questions on which the average citizen must make up his mind to vote intelligently. It matters little whether a community round table discussing such a problem reaches agreement or not. Discussion is successful if it has helped the individual member to understand the problem, to clarify his thinking on it, and to reach a settled opinion with which he is personally satisfied. The public policy which the citizen is invited to approve or disapprove or the policies among which he is invited to choose have already been formulated, usually by a legislative committee. The object of discussion is individual decision on policy rather than group formulation of policy.

By a problem of personal conduct is not meant a particular problem encountered by a single individual, but one which nearly every individual encounters in his daily life as businessman, parent, or citizen. A few examples will illustrate the type:

What should be my attitude at Conway High School toward Negroes in my classes? As a mother how should I deal with the untruthful child? As a businessman what should be my attitude toward the outside union organizer? As a high school teacher how should I deal with the discipline problem in my classroom? How late should teen-age children stay out on school nights? What arrangement should a family make for an elderly relative who has no means of support?

Life is a succession of personal and family problems of this sort. With due allowance for variation in circumstances, the problems are much the same for all individuals. And people of all sorts find it profitable to explore them at the conference table. The object of discussion is not to formulate policy on which the group will act collectively or to help the individual make up his mind on public policy formulated in Washington. It is to help the individual understand better a problem he must often encounter and to arrive at general principles by which to guide his own conduct.

Problems of the last type are more provocative of discussion when stated concretely. Often the discussion leader, drawing on his own experience, observation, or imagination, can construct a typical case which presents the problem in dramatic form. In opening a discussion by a parent–teacher association of the parent's responsibility in connection with truancy, he might present in story form a truancy case bristling with challenging questions and then invite discussion of the question: What would you have done if you had been this child's mother? Most people react more vigorously to a concrete situation presenting a problem than to an abstract statement of a topic. The situation presented must of course be close to the experience of the group, so that each recognizes in it a problem similar to those he encounters in his own life.

Sources of Information

In one respect the following passage is typical of all discussion:

Moderator: Apparently you all agree that the United Nations does not go far enough and that we need a true world government. But you also agree that Russia probably would not go along on such a proposal. How, then, are you to get world government?

Mrs. Dorne: One possibility is to scrap the UN and set up a world government without Russia.

Mr. Cartwright: But it's always bad to scrap a going concern. In the end you may get nothing in its place. Wouldn't it make more sense to strengthen the UN in the direction of world government?

Mrs. Swift: On general principles I would agree. But you could convert the UN into a world government only by elaborately amending the Charter. Can that be done if Russia opposes it?

Moderator: That is a question of fact. Let's examine Article 109, which lays down the procedure for amending the Charter.

Mr. Cartwright: Here it is. Article 109 reads as follows: . . .

This exchange is typical of all discussion in that questions of two sorts arise. One is a question of principle, or value: Is it wise to scrap an existing institution? The second is a question of fact: Can the Charter be amended if Russia opposes amendment? All differences of opinion arise over questions either of principle or of fact, and most of the contributions made in discussion are statements of principle or of fact. A disputed question of principle may be settled by the analysis, criticism, and eventual modification of the opposing views. But difference over a question of fact cannot be resolved without the fact. The discussion quoted above would soon have reached a dead end if the necessary fact had not been available.

It is an essential condition of profitable discussion that information be available. Without it the group will either waste its time in idle speculation or will be obliged to shelve one disputed question of fact after another with the result that no conclusion can be reached.

In discussing problems of personal conduct much of the necessary information is common knowledge. A group of mothers, for example, might profitably discuss a problem in the handling of children on the basis of their own experience and observation—though information from a child psychologist would undoubtedly improve the discussion. But in considering most problems the group will need more information than it already possesses if discussion is to be worth while, and provision must be made in advance for making the information available. This may be done in any one of four ways.

The Rosedale Women's Club is composed for the most part of women with the time and inclination to do serious reading in preparation for their discussion of universal military training. Two weeks in advance of the meeting each member receives a brief bibliography of books and articles on the subject available in the local library. Members appear at the meeting reasonably well informed and in many cases armed with printed material to which they can refer in the course of discussion.

But the Rosedale Women's Club is a serious study group. The chairman of the Businessmen's Club has found that few members of the club have time to prepare thoroughly for discussion. If the group is to consider military training, it will be well to ask several of the members who have time for it either to present brief factual reports on the problem before discussion is attempted, or to have information at hand on particular points likely to come up in the discussion. Such reports are more likely to be useful if the member is given a list of available sources of information to consult and if it is suggested that what is wanted from him primarily is an impartial statement of fact rather than an expression of opinion.

In some cases one or more persons qualified to speak as experts on the subject can be invited to attend the meeting. A community council considering a recreational program for the community, for example, might arrange to have the heads of social agencies in the town participate in the discussion or attend as expert witnesses to supply information. It should always be made clear to such resource persons, as they are called, what will be expected of them. Otherwise they may monopolize the conversation and so overawe the laymen in the group that no real discussion is possible.

Frequently the discussion leader himself must be the chief source of information for the group. While he will seldom be an expert on the subject, and it is not necessary that he should be, the better informed he is, the more useful he will be. He should be prepared to open the discussion with a ten- or fifteen-minute factual statement, laying a foundation on which discussion can proceed; and so far as possible he should be ready to supply additional items of information as needed during discussion.

All members of the group, then, may study the problem in advance, several of them may prepare reports for the information of the group, experts may be called in to testify, or the leader himself may undertake to supply information. But in one way or another the information necessary for intelligent consideration of the problem must be made available if discussion is to serve its purpose.

To summarize the suggestions of this chapter, discussion is unlikely to be profitable unless care has been taken in advance to ensure conditions favorable to group thinking. Suitable physical arrangements and provision for adequate time must be made; the group must be of the right size and properly constituted, and it must approach its work with a sound conception of what group thinking is; the problem must be suitable for discussion by the particular group; and there must be provision for making the necessary information available. Given these conditions, the stage is set for a profitable session; without them the most skillful leadership will be of little avail.

References

Braden, Waldo W. and Earnest Brandenburg, *Oral Decision-Making,* New York: Harper & Row, Publishers, 1955, Chap. 15.

McBurney, James H. and Kenneth G. Hance, *Discussion in Human Affairs,* New York: Harper & Row, Publishers, 1950, Chap. 5.

CHAPTER 3

Preparing for Discussion

Pooling ignorance does not produce wisdom. As observed in the preceding chapter, one condition of profitable discussion is adequate information on the question discussed. On some of the practical problems considered by committees and administrative boards and on some of those discussed by community organizations the necessary information is already common knowledge; on others it can be obtained only by calling in experts. But on most state, national, and international questions information must be sought in the library. Those preparing for discussion of such topics, whether as participants or moderators, should be willing to do serious reading.

General Information

To participate effectively in discussion of controversial public questions one needs a general knowledge of current events as well as information on the specific topic. This background cannot be acquired hastily; it is the cumulative product of regular and thoughtful newspaper reading. Even the regular reading of a good Sunday edition soon gives one the feeling that he knows at least in a general way who is who and what is what in the world of public affairs. Especially useful is Section 4 of the Sunday *New York Times*, devoted to a review of news of the week. Incidentally, a file of this section of the *Times* is extremely useful when one wishes to "get up" on a particular topic. By glancing through the file for the last month or two one can piece together a dependable account of what has been happening in connection with almost any topic of public interest.

Without a general background of information the participant in discussion is betrayed constantly into minor inaccuracies in statement of fact that make him sound ill informed even when he has spent considerable time in study of the topic. Those wishing to discuss public questions should make thoughtful newspaper reading a habit.

Reading on the Problem

Usually one must also inform himself on the topic to be discussed. Of the many available sources of information one of the most useful is the university or public library. If the topic has long been under discussion, books on it may be available. The reader should consult the card-index catalog of books in the library, and should not hesitate to ask the librarian to help. An acquaintance with the controversial literature on both sides of the question will be helpful, but what one needs especially is factual information; so the more impartial sources should primarily be consulted.

On many topics of current interest newspapers and magazines will be the chief source of information. Libraries subscribe to the more important magazines, and most of them take several daily newspapers. *The New York Times*, the standard newspaper for reference work in this country, will be found in nearly all libraries. To find what is available in the magazines, the *Reader's Guide to Periodical Literature* may be consulted. This index lists magazine articles alphabetically by subject, author, and title. *The New York Times Index* provides a comparable guide to news articles, editorials, and special articles appearing in that newspaper.

Much informational material is distributed free, or at a nominal cost, by governmental and private agencies. For example, the "Headline Series" of pamphlets and the "Foreign Policy Reports" are issued by the Foreign Policy Association, at 345 E. 46th Street, New York 17, N.Y. The League of Women Voters of the United States, 1026 17th Street, N.W., Washington 6, D.C., publishes pamphlet material on many public questions. The American Association for the United Nations and the Commission to Study the Organization of Peace, both with headquarters at 345 E. 46th Street, New York 17, N.Y., publish material on international affairs and the work of the United Nations. Perhaps the best single source of current information on activities of the United Nations is the *United Nations Review* published by the office of Public Information, the United Nations, New York, N.Y. *The Congressional Digest,* published at 3231 P Street, N.W., Washington 7, D.C., contains information and comment on questions pending in Congress.

The Research Document

As one studies a problem, he accumulates a store of information and argument likely to be useful in discussion. Much of it will be promptly forgotten unless he takes notes. Obviously a notebook filled with unorganized jottings will be of little use at the conference table. Notes taken on 3 x 5 index cards can be arranged under a set of headings and are more convenient to use.

Perhaps still more convenient is a document in which one has organized for ready reference the information and evidence accumulated during his study of the problem. Such a statement cannot of course be followed in discussion as a speaker might follow an outline in delivering a public address; it is to be thought of rather as a storehouse of information and argument which the participant may wish to consult from time to time during discussion as need for particular items of information arises.

A convenient form for this statement is illustrated below. The introduction contains in outline form a statement of the question, definitions, expository material, and the agenda which the participant believes should be followed in discussion. At the beginning of its deliberation the group may of course agree upon a different statement of the question, and following the procedure suggested in Chapter 4, may arrive at a somewhat different agenda.

The issues listed in the agenda provide section headings for the argumentative material in the body of the document. This material should be briefed (a process to be explained presently) and arranged in two columns, that in the first column supporting an affirmative answer to the issue, that in the second column, a negative answer. In the complete statement argument would be similarly arranged under the other two issues also.

The third division of this document lists the student's principal sources of information. These bibliographical notes should be sufficiently detailed and accurate so that another person could quickly find in a library the material listed.

INTRODUCTION

I. Question: Should federal lobbies be further regulated?

II. Definitions:

    A. A "lobby" is a paid staff maintained in Washington by any group for the purpose of influencing legislation in the interest of the group.

    B. By "regulation" is meant regulation by federal law.

III. Exposition:

    A. At present lobbies are regulated only by the Legislative Reorganization Act.

    B. This act provides that

        1. The lobbyist must register with the clerk of the House and the secretary of the Senate;

        2. He must state who employs him;

3. He must reveal the amount of his salary and living allowance.

IV. Agenda:

    A. Does the lobby affect American political life favorably?
    B. Does the Legislative Reorganization Act sufficiently guard against the harmful effects of lobbying?
    C. What further regulatory legislation would be desirable?

BODY

I. Does the lobby affect American political life favorably?

A. The lobbyist assists Congress in drafting legislation, for

    1. He can inform Congress on the subjects covered by legislation, for

        a. He is an expert on the subject of his interest, and

        b. He can employ a research staff to assist him, and

        c. He is kept informed by his interest group regarding its needs.

    2. He can often give Congress expert advice on the technical details of drafting legislation, for

        a. He often has legal training, and

        b. He knows in detail how legislation will affect his interest group.

A. Congress needs no assistance from the lobbyist in drafting legislation, for

    1. Legislative committees can summon experts to testify before them, and

    2. Most congressmen have had legal training.

B. Lobbying often results in legislation contrary to the public interest, for

    1. The interest of the lobbyist's employing group is often contrary to the public interest, and

    2. The lobbyist can win legislative support for the measure he advocates, for

        a. He has personal access to members of Congress, while

        b. The public has no comparable means of making its influence felt.

C. The methods of the lobbyist are sometimes objectionable, for

    1. He may use large sums of money for lavish entertainment, and

2. He can finance an avalanche of telegrams and letters to congressmen purporting to come from the public.

II. Does the Legislative Reorganization Act sufficiently guard against the harmful effects of lobbying? etc.

BIBLIOGRAPHY

"Save the Lobbies," *The Commonweal,* January 9, 1948, p. 316.

Tris Coffin, "No Speech Ever Changed a Vote," *New Republic,* July 14, 1947, p. 16.

Nathan Strauss, "Why You Can't Get That New Home," *American Magazine,* December, 1947, p. 21.

Nancy Mayo Waterman, "Pressure Groups in Action," *Forum,* December, 1946, p. 514.

"Ending Secrecy of Lobbies," *United States News,* August 9, 1946, p. 16.

"About Rules for Lobbyists," *United States News,* August 16, 1946, p. 48.

"Who Foots the Bill for Lobbyists?" *Business Week,* January 18, 1947, p. 18.

"New Style Lobbying Tactics," *United States News,* August 29, 1947, p. 15.

Carlisle Bargeron, "They Don't Wear Tails and Horns," *Nation's Business,* November, 1947, p. 42.

Marshall E. and Gladys O. Dimock, *American Government in Action,* New York: Holt, Rinehart and Winston, Inc., 1951, Chap. 25.

Peter Odegard and E. A. Helms, "Pressure Politics and Majority Rule," *American Politics,* New York: Harper and Row, Publishers, 1947, Chap. 22.

V. O. Key, "The Role and Techniques of Pressure Groups," *Politics, Parties and Pressure Groups,* 4th ed. New York: Thomas Y. Crowell Co., 1958. Chap. 6.

A. N. Christensen and E. M. Kirkpatrick, "In Defense of Lobbying," and "The Regulation of Lobbying," *The People, Politics, and the Politician,* New York: Holt, Rinehart and Winston, Inc., 1941, pp. 412–431.

Stuart Chase, *Democracy under Pressure,* New York: The Twentieth Century Fund, Inc., 1945, pp. 119–121.

Briefing Argument

It has been recommended that in the body of the research document the material in each of the parallel columns be briefed rather than written out in paragraph form. To reduce to briefed form a paragraph of argumentative material in an article or a speech, first strip away the illustrations, repetitions, and other material designed to make the argument more interesting or persuasive and phrase the remaining material as a series of short declarative sentences, each expressing one of the points of which the argument is composed. If these statements are arranged in the form of a chart in such a way as to make clear at a glance the relation of each point to every other point and to the argument as a whole, the argument has been briefed. The statements now appear as heads and subheads, each expressing one point only, and each is phrased as a declarative sentence. The statements are so arranged that each helps to prove the truth of the statement to which it is subordinate. A system of notation (symbols) and of indentation is used consistently to indicate the relationship of subordination. The principal rules to be followed in briefing argument might be summarized as follows:

1. Each point should be expressed in a simple declarative sentence.
2. Only one point should be expressed in each statement.
3. The statements should be so arranged that each helps to prove the truth of the statement to which it is subordinate.
4. A system of notation and indentation should be employed consistently.

By way of illustration consider the following paragraph:

Among other things the United Nations is a modern Tower of Babel. While the UN has five official languages, no one of them is spoken by all of the delegates or ever will be. They are too difficult to learn. Each delegate speaks in one or another of the five languages, pausing every few minutes while a crew of expert linguists translate what has been said into the other four languages. All delegates wear earphones, and those not understanding the speaker's language tune in on the language of his choice as it comes to him from the booth of the appropriate interpreter. Then the speaker continues for a few more minutes and pauses again until the interpreters have caught up. The process is interesting to watch but very time consuming. In this connection some attention has been given to the use in the UN of Interlingua, one of the best of the auxiliary international languages. It has the great advantage of being very easy to learn. Its vocabulary consists primarily of words already common to several of the national languages, and its grammar is very simple. As a matter of fact anyone speaking one of the occidental languages will find that he can read Interlingua reasonably well without ever having studied it at all. The United Nations would do well to adopt Interlingua as one of its official languages.

This paragraph can be briefed as follows:

I. The United Nations should adopt Interlingua as an official auxiliary language, for
  A. A single language used by all delegates would greatly facilitate communication, for
    1. The use of interpreters is time consuming, and
    2. No one of the national languages will ever be used by all delegates, for
      a. They are too difficult to learn.
  B. Interlingua is easy to learn, for
    1. Its grammar is very simple, and
    2. Its vocabulary consists primarily of words already common to several languages.

It will be noted that the argument in the parallel columns of the sample research statement quoted above is briefed. This form greatly reduces the bulk of the document and makes the argument easy to understand at a glance.

CHAPTER 4

Pattern in
Discussion

When conducted under favorable conditions discussion is usually lively and interesting. In some situations nothing more is desired. But most groups have a definite purpose. The committee, the staff meeting, or the community council has a problem to solve; so does the neighborhood round table, though it may make little difference whether it reaches agreement on a solution. Not content with intellectual amusement, such groups have a destination in view and wish to arrive there as surely and expeditiously as possible.

A group setting out on the troubled and sometimes treacherous sea of discussion without a map to guide it is unlikely to reach any destination, however interesting the expedition may prove. It will drift haphazardly from one aspect of the problem to another, wasting much time in repetitious and irrelevant remarks and failing in the end to consider some phase of the problem essential to a sound solution. Much committee discussion is of this kind. It affords a lively exchange of views but produces no such change of views as would make agreement possible, and often it reveals little awareness of what those crucial points are upon which decision logically should turn.

What the group needs is a map of the territory to be covered, indicating the boundaries within which discussion is to be confined and subdividing the area to be explored. Typically the map consists of a series of questions to be taken up in turn and to which the group will seek answers as it searches for a solution of the problem. In some cases the questions can themselves be broken down into subordinate questions.

At least three different kinds of pattern, each serving a different purpose, may prove useful: pattern to insure relevance, pattern to avoid confusion, and pattern to facilitate the resolution of especially difficult conflicts of opinion. Each will be considered in turn.

Pattern to Insure Relevance: The Agenda

To reach a rational solution of its problem the group must talk about the right things; that is, it must consider and reach a decision on each of the issues on which logically decision should turn. A statement of these issues in interrogative form we shall refer to as the agenda. Often the group's first task is to work out such a set of issues and subordinate issues to be examined in turn during the discussion. And if the problem is a complex one, the task is too important to be hurried. When four or five sessions are to be devoted to the problem, all of the first may be needed for this spade work. For the issues cannot simply be picked out of the air; they must be based on analysis of the problem. In this connection it is useful to think of the total process of problem solving as involving a series of steps, in connection with each of which the group may need to raise a number of questions as it searches for an agenda. Each step will here be considered in turn.

1. LOCATING THE PROBLEM. When a group sits down to discuss a problem, it might be presumed that it is clear what the problem is and that it is the business of this group to solve it. In real life situations, this is not always the case. Sometimes the group does well to consider at this early stage three questions:

a. Does the situation that confronts us really present a problem? We are aware, for example, that the situation in regard to student housing on the campus is not altogether satisfactory. But is it serious enough to present a real problem? Do the dormitories now under construction promise a solution without further action? If so, why discuss the matter? If convinced that a real problem exists, the group may next raise the question:

b. To whom is the problem presented? As the executive committee of the YMCA on campus, we are interested in student housing; but is student housing properly our responsibility? Would the problem be considered more appropriately by a committee of the faculty? Or if students are to express themselves on the matter in a communication to the faculty, would the student senate be the more appropriate body to take this action? Failure to consider this question may sometimes lead a group to meddle in what is not its proper concern or, on the other hand, to fail to take action when action would be desirable. If the matter is properly a problem for this group,

c. What exactly is the problem? Usually the group does well to state the problem interrogatively and in as specific terms as can be done without risking the exclusion from consideration of what is really a part of the problem. In general the more narrowly the problem is defined, the better. At this stage the group may go through a process of narrowing the problem. The question, What should be done about the housing situation? is replaced by the more specific question, What should the YMCA do to improve housing? And this finally is rephrased as follows: Should the YMCA conduct a poll among male students living off campus to determine the adequacy of off-campus living accommodations?

At this point it may be useful to observe that the question to be discussed may finally be stated in terms of the problem itself, in terms of the specific objective to be achieved by any solution adopted, or in terms of some one solution. In preparing to discuss public health, for example, a group may state the question in any one of the following forms: What should be done about the public health situation? (statement in terms of the problem). How can medical services best be made available to all who need them? (statement in terms of the objective). Should Congress pass the Caldwell bill? (statement in terms of a specific solution). In all three forms the problem (public health) is the same, but the specific question to be discussed differs. In which form the question should be stated depends, as the following pages will show, on the result of the group's analysis of the problem.

2. ANALYZING THE PROBLEM. In its search for an agenda the group often should raise and answer four questions under the general head of analyzing the problem:

a. On what assumptions, if any, must the problem be solved? It is sometimes virtually impossible to discuss a problem without making one or more assumptions, that is, without accepting as true what the group cannot be certain is actually true. For example, it is next to impossible to discuss the problem of U.S. policy toward the Union of South Africa without assuming that the Union either will or will not continue its present policy of Apartheid. A group discussing the problem may feel that continuance of the policy is highly probable, but it cannot be quite sure of this. It therefore assumes that the policy will be continued and discusses the problem on that basis. Any such assumption should of course be as probably true as possible. And the group should always make an assumption reluctantly, for every assumption made qualifies the solution finally reached; that is, the best that can be said for the solution is that it will be sound if the assumption is true.

b. On what conditions, if any, must the problem be solved? Frequently the resources available for solution of the problem, in terms for example of time, money, or manpower, are limited, and this fact can be known in advance. And occasionally previous commitments, legal or otherwise, set limits within which the solution must be found. A staff of executives considering an improvement in a method of utilizing the secretarial staff may know in advance that no solution is acceptable that would increase the wage bill or violate the firm's contract with the union. If such conditions circumscribe the area within which a solution must be sought, they should be kept in mind from the beginning.

c. What are the causes of the problem? In the course of analysis it is often useful to consider why the problem has arisen. Before proceeding far with discussion of juvenile delinquency, for example, it may be well to examine the circumstances that lead young people into antisocial behavior. Probably many factors contribute to the result, some of them associated with the home, some with the community. To identify these factors and to arrange them in intelligible order helps to clarify thinking on the problem.

d. By what criteria should solutions be evaluated? In the course of its discussion the group will examine and evaluate one or more possible solutions of the problem. No agreement on a solution is likely unless in evaluating the possibilities all members are measuring the solutions by the same yardstick. It is therefore desirable that the group agree upon the criteria before attempting to discuss solutions. It sharpens thinking at this point to raise the question in this form: What must the solution do (or in some cases, not do) if it is to solve the problem satisfactorily? Usually listing the criteria amounts to stating the objectives the solution must achieve to be acceptable; occasionally it amounts rather to listing the values to be conserved, the difficulties to be removed, or the favorable conditions to be created by the solution. A group discussing Problem No. 62 in the appendix of this volume, for example, might agree on the following criteria: the solution should (a) result in prompt resumption of production, (b) discourage similar work stoppages in the future, and (c) not be unfair to the Witnesses. There is often room for difference of opinion on what the criteria should be, but if the group can agree on them in advance, it is more likely to agree on a solution.

3. GATHERING DATA. Often the information necessary for profitable discussion is already in the group's possession. Or, as suggested in Chapter 2, it may be made available by special resource persons, by a few members of the group who study the problem in advance, or perhaps by the moderator himself. But occasionally much more is needed. Indeed extensive research may be necessary before the group can get far with its problem, and a series of sessions with opportunity for research between them may be advisable. Before attempting to gather data it may be wise for the group to raise such questions as the following: What data

will be needed? Where can the data be obtained? How can the data, when collected, be made most intelligible? By arranging it in outline or tabular form? By putting it on paper in the form of maps, charts, diagrams, or graphs? A final question usually worth raising at this point is: How reliable are the data? That is, how impartial and how well qualified as authorities are the persons from whom the facts are obtained?

4. PROJECTING POSSIBLE SOLUTIONS. Frequently it is obvious to the group what are the possible solutions from which a choice must be made. In discussing a presidential campaign, for example, the choice for most members will be between two major candidates. Or the problem has been long under public discussion and the practicable alternatives have already been narrowed down to three or four; from these a choice must be made. But in other situations it may be far from clear what the alternatives are; indeed the problem may be a new one for which solutions have never been proposed. In this case the group must formulate possible solutions before it can evaluate them.

When the development of solutions for examination presents serious difficulty, the group may find it useful to devote twenty minutes or so to "brain storming" the problem in its search for possible solutions. "Brain storming" is a special procedure recommended and popularized by Mr. Alex F. Osborn[1] when the sole task of the group, at least for the moment, is to originate new ideas for later examination. During such a session the moderator should follow the following four rules, or principles: (a) critical comment, favorable or unfavorable, on the ideas suggested is ruled out, (b) any idea is welcome, no matter how absurd it may sound, (c) the more ideas suggested during the session the better, and (d) ideas which combine, elaborate, or improve upon ideas already suggested are welcome. Except for observing these rules, the session is conducted very informally, all members speaking up promptly the moment ideas occur to them. A twenty-minute session will often produce sixty or more ideas. Upon subsequent examination some of them will prove to be duplicates of others,

[1] *Applied Imagination*, New York: Charles Scribner's Sons, 1961.

and many may prove to be without merit; but among those suggested are likely to be at least a few of value. The rules followed, especially the one forbidding critical comment, encourages a more spontaneous and creative use of the imagination than is usually possible when the group attempts to combine invention and criticism of ideas in the same session.

In any case the group will usually save time and be more productive if it lists in order the solutions to be examined before attempting to evaluate any of them.

5. SELECTING THE BEST SOLUTION. As it undertakes a detailed examination of the possible solutions, the group will of course raise such questions as the following: How well does each solution satisfy the criteria? How well does each meet the conditions under which the problem must be solved? How difficult will it be to implement each solution? And finally, everything considered, which is the best solution?

6. IMPLEMENTING THE SOLUTION. In some cases it is a part of the group's task to decide what steps must be taken to put the solution into operation. If so, a consideration of implementation will be the final step in the group's consideration of its problem.

The preceding pages may have seemed to imply that in its search for an agenda a group should always go through all of the six steps in the problem-solving sequence and in the order indicated. Neither is true. The order of the steps may sometimes be varied to advantage. For example, it may sometimes be necessary to collect at least some data before considering location of the problem or to go back and reconsider location of the problem after data has been collected. Or it may be desirable to project possible solutions before determining the criteria. The most that can be said is that the order of steps indicated is usually convenient. Nor need the group always go through all six steps as it works out an agenda. In some cases it may be perfectly obvious that the situation presents a problem which this group must solve and equally obvious what the problem is—the first step may be omitted. In analysis of the problem perhaps only the determination of criteria requires attention. It may be unnecessary to collect data or to provide for implementation of the solution chosen. In fact in simple situations the series of steps may reduce to the following four questions: What is the problem? What are the criteria? What are the possible solutions? In the light of the criteria which solution is best? In a particular case perhaps not even all of these questions need to be raised.

One further comment on the use of the steps in the problem-solving sequence may be in order. The six steps, with the subordinate questions proposed under each, are best thought of as a pattern for use in working out an agenda rather than as the actual agenda itself to be followed in discussion. Let us suppose that a group will discuss the question: Should the federal government provide financial aid to the state school systems? In a preliminary session it may quickly become apparent that there is already complete agreement regarding what the problem is and regarding the facts out of which it arises: that in many parts of the country school facilities and staff are inadequate because of the inability of the state to finance its schools properly. All are agreed also that the only proposal to be considered is that of federal aid, that its objective is to strengthen the school systems of the states, and that the objective is a sound one. The only question, therefore, on which there is a difference of opinion is whether federal aid would be a satisfactory way to achieve the objective.

Discussion has also made clear that in approaching this question the group will encounter two principal areas of disagreement: (1) Would federal aid actually strengthen the school systems of the states by providing better facilities and staffs? and (2) Is the proposal open to serious objection on grounds apart from whether it would achieve its objective? Would it, for example, involve a dangerous degree of political control of education? And would it be unfair to the wealthier states?

As a result of its preliminary analysis, the group might well adopt the following as the agenda to be followed in discussion:

1. Would federal aid actually strengthen the school systems of the various states?

    a. Would it provide adequate facilities?

    b. Would it provide an adequate staff of well-trained teachers?

2. Is the proposal open to serious objection on other grounds?

    a. Would it involve a dangerous degree of political control of education?

    b. Would it be unfair to the wealthier states to tax their residents for the support of education in other states?

If the group can answer these questions to its satisfaction, it will have made up its mind on the wisdom of federal aid to education.

It thus is clear that working out an agenda involves a preliminary exploration both of the problem and of the present beliefs of the group about the problem. The group's purpose during its preliminary discussion is to arrive at those issues that must be settled to reach a decision, and the agenda is a statement in interrogative form of these controversial issues. When a satisfactory agenda has been adopted, the group has a pattern to follow that will ensure relevance in discussion.

Pattern to Avoid Confusion in Discussion

The necessity of working out an agenda is not peculiar to group thinking. An individual attempting to solve a problem alone must understand what issues are involved before he can examine and weigh the evidence. And if the suggestions of the preceding section of this chapter are useful to a group, they presumably are useful also to the individual thinker.

But when a group has an agenda before it and is ready to discuss the first issue, it encounters a problem peculiar to group thinking—the problem of how several persons are to think together. One virtue in group thinking is that many minds are brought to bear on the problem. Many minds mean many ideas, and many ideas should produce a sounder conclusion than few ideas. But many ideas may also produce confusion unless the group avoids trying to think about all of them at the same time. Yet this is what most groups do. As the group takes up one of the issues in its agenda, the members speak up in turn, each contributing information, suggestions, and arguments, some agreeing and some disagreeing with what others have said. As each speaks, the situation becomes more involved. Soon so many points have been made and so many reactions have been expressed to each that no one can remember what anyone else has said. The first contribution, like a pebble dropped into a pond, has set up an area of agitation that widens rapidly in all directions until soon the eye cannot take it in.

What the group needs is a method of conducting its discussion that will help each member to keep the total situation in mind as it evolves and that will enable the group to concentrate on one idea at a time. The following sequence of four steps to be followed in discussing an issue will enable a group to avoid much of the confusion that often embarrasses group thinking: (1) exploring the issue, (2) taking stock of the situation, (3) resolving disagreements, (4) summarizing the discussion.

1. EXPLORING THE ISSUE. As suggested above, the tendency of any group to make contributions in a random and spontaneous fashion without any attempt to keep the situation clear, to sort out the ideas presented, or to stick to any one of them long soon results in confusion. Yet some discussion of this kind is necessary as the group takes up each new issue. For the situation with which the group must deal consists in part of the relationship between views of the various members on the issue. Some of the ideas presented will supplement one another and can be fitted into a harmonious pattern; others will be contradictory. Until each member has expressed himself briefly, the group cannot know what situation confronts it.

At the beginning of the discussion of each issue, then, the members should speak up in rapid succession, each stating his view, perhaps indicating briefly why he believes as he does, perhaps also commenting briefly on the views expressed by other members. We shall call this the "exploratory phase" of the discussion. Its purpose is to make clear what the situation is at the beginning of the group's thinking about the issue. To accomplish this purpose may require only two or three minutes; seldom should it require more than twenty. The mistake of many groups is to continue too long in this phase.

During the exploratory phase the group may find that the issue is too broad for convenient handling and that it would be desirable to break it down into two or more subordinate issues. If so, the first of the subordinate issues becomes the issue to be explored. When discussion of this issue has been carried through to a conclusion, the group returns to exploration of the second subordinate issue, and so on.

To illustrate the exploratory phase and subsequent steps in the discussion of an issue let us suppose that a committee representing the village band in the town of Dorchester has met to consider how new life can be instilled into the organization. Earlier in the discussion it has been agreed that what the band needs to revive the interest of its members is new music, a more satisfactory practice room, and several new instruments, and that the problem is essentially one of raising six or seven hundred dollars for these purposes. As we look in on the meeting, the committee is taking up the issue, Could the money be raised by giving a public concert in the spring?

Dale: A public concert seems to me a good thing quite apart from its money-making possibilities. It would do a great deal to give the band standing in the community and in surrounding communities.

Dennis: I think it would, and with a concert to look forward to, we'd all dig in and practice. We need something like that to make us buckle down.

Marcussen: That may all be true enough, and I agree with you, but a public concert is a pretty ambitious project. We might clear the $600 we need—and we might lose several hundred. Have you thought of that?

Royer: Frankly I think we'd be biting off more than we can chew. We'd have to sell six or eight hundred tickets at around a dollar apiece. That means you'd have to sell a good many out of town. We are just not that good, or if we are nobody knows it.

Dennis: I take it Royer and Marcussen think it would be a good idea if we could swing it. (Royer and Marcussen nod assent.) Then I think we ought to give it some real consideration. "Faint heart ne'er won fair lady," as the old woman said.

Dale: I can see that we would have to sell a good many tickets out of town, and I'm beginning to feel a little dubious about it myself. But still—

At this point the exploratory phase of the discussion by the committee should be closed. It is clear about where each member stands on the issue, and the group should proceed to the second step in their discussion before the picture becomes confused.

2. TAKING STOCK OF THE SITUATION. When it has become clear where each member stands on the issue, it should be possible to sort the ideas presented into three groups. In the first group fall those on which there is complete agreement. These points of agreement should be formulated clearly and set aside as requiring no further discussion; to return to them continually, as groups often do, is a waste of time. In the second group fall those points on which the members are unable to come to any opinion at all because they lack the information necessary to form an opinion. If the group believes the information could be obtained, these points should be set aside for discussion at a future date when the information can be made available. To discuss them now will serve no purpose. In the third group fall those points on which there is a difference of opinion. These points of disagreement should be stated clearly, so that they can be taken up in order and threshed out thoroughly. The process of taking stock is thus essentially one of classifying the material presented in the exploratory phase of the discussion.

The exploratory discussion may of course reveal no points of agreement; it may reveal no points on which lack of information makes the formation of opinion impossible; or it may reveal no points of disagreement. If all members find themselves in complete agreement, the group will of course proceed at once to the next issue in the agenda.

Frequently when it is time to take stock of the situation it may not be perfectly clear whether there is disagreement on a particular point. If so, the chairman, or some member, should put a direct question to the member about whose opinion there is doubt to make sure whether disagreement exists.

In the committee discussion we are here using as an illustration, the stock-taking process is a simple one:

Dennis: I wonder if we can't clear the air a little before we get any deeper into the discussion. Just how do we stand on this?

Dale: The situation is about this, isn't it? We are agreed that giving a public concert would have the advantages of building up the band's reputation and of providing a needed incentive to do better work. But we are disagreed over whether it would be possible to raise the six hundred dollars in this way.

3. RESOLVING DISAGREEMENTS. As the group takes up in turn each of the points on which there is difference of opinion, it will need a sense of method if any progress is to be made in resolving the conflicts. Too often what happens is that each of the two members in disagreement simply restates and again restates his view with mounting emphasis, and what began as a conflict of opinion degenerates into a conflict of will. Acrimonious repetition of what has already been said never resolves a disagreement.

The chance of reaching agreement is often good, however, if the two members at odds can be brought to present their supporting reasons step by step and to criticize each other's reasons as they do so. Suppose, for example, that Smith and Brown are in disagreement. Brown, instead of repeating his point, gives one of the main reasons why he thinks as he does. Smith replies with a criticism of the reason. To this Brown replies by commenting on Smith's reaction to his argument.

This mutual criticism of each other's supporting arguments usually produces two useful results. For one thing, it soon makes clear just why Brown and Smith disagree, and this is worth while even when no further progress can be made. But often further progress is possible. For soon Brown is likely to say, "I see Smith has a real objection there. I don't think it applies to what I meant to say. I'm afraid I didn't express myself very clearly. Let me put my point this way." And he restates his position, retaining the gist of what he meant to say but freeing it somewhat from Smith's objection. Actually he usually is modifying his position, though he may not realize it.

And Smith, too, is likely to say soon, "I think my objection to Brown's point sounded a little more sweeping than I intended. What I meant was this." And he restates his own position, consciously or unconsciously modifying it as he does so. This progressive modification of the opposing positions brings the two members closer and closer together. More often than one might expect, it brings them completely together. And when complete agreement cannot be achieved, it is often possible to narrow the area of disagreement to a single disputed question of fact with a fair prospect that when the fact is found, complete agreement will result.

This process of examining the supporting arguments back of a conflict of opinion may be illustrated from the committee discussion of the proposed band concert in Dorchester:

Marcussen: Why do I think we can't do it? Because it is clear we would have to sell six or eight hundred tickets, many of them out of town, and I don't think the band has that much appeal. Our free open-air concerts during the summer are well attended locally. But I don't think we have enough to offer to attract many from out of town.

Dennis: Maybe not if the concert is to consist entirely of band numbers, but couldn't we have a few added attractions that would draw?

Marcussen: What, for instance?

Dennis: For one thing, suppose we hire for the occasion three or four players from the City Symphony Orchestra to fill in at certain points where we are admittedly weak, say a solo trumpet, a trombone, and two good clarinetists to strengthen the reed section. With this help we could present some classical or semiclassical numbers that would be something new around here.

Dale: If we are to bring in outside help, how about a few solo numbers? Mrs. Corey lives right here in the village. I imagine we could get her to present a soprano solo with band accompaniment. I know she is interested in the band, and I think she would help and not charge us too much either.

Marcussen: I'll admit this looks pretty good. If we bring in Mrs. Corey and several professionals from the city, we'd have something that would appeal. But this will cost a couple of hundred dollars, I suppose. Now you'll have to sell a thousand tickets!

Dennis: I think we could do it.

Royer: Maybe so. I'd go along if I were sure we could get the outside help for, say, not more than two hundred dollars.

Marcussen: I'd agree, too, I think, on those terms.

Dale: Then why not have Marcussen, our business manager, see what it would cost to put on such a concert?

4. SUMMARIZING THE DISCUSSION. When all points of disagreement have been threshed out thoroughly, the chairman should sum up the discussion. The summary should not be a tedious review of the arguments presented but a brief statement of the results of the discussion. After restating the issue that has been under discussion, the chairman should enumerate the points on which the group was agreed at the end of the exploratory phase; he should enumerate the points on which the members were undecided because information was lacking and mention what provision has been made to obtain the needed information; and he should enumerate the points of disagreement encountered and the progress, if any, made in resolving the conflicts. The entire summary should seldom require more than three or four sentences.

In the illustration being followed here the summary might run as follows:

Dale: On this question of whether the needed money could be raised by a public concert in the spring, then, what we have arrived at is this: We are agreed that such a concert would have the advantages of building up the reputation of the band and providing an incentive to the members. There was at first some disagreement over whether the money could be raised by a concert, but the committee now believes the proposal would be feasible if the outside help we would need did not cost too much. Marcussen is to find out what it would cost to put on a concert with this outside help.

Group thinking would be greatly facilitated if all members of the group kept in mind the series of steps outlined here. Most people find it difficult to do this while immersed in discussion, and in actual practice a group depends a good deal on the guidance of its moderator. In a later chapter we shall return to the problem while discussing the function of the moderator in group thinking.

Special Pattern—When Difference of Opinion Is Acute

Situations sometimes arise in which it is important to reach agreement on an issue but in which the group is divided by a difference of opinion so deep seated and acute that progress toward consensus seems almost impossible. Occasionally not one issue in the agenda only but the problem as a whole presents this difficulty. A community council composed of white and Negro leaders in the South meeting to consider the problem of integration of the public schools might find itself so divided. In such situations it may be desirable to abandon the patterns usually followed in conference and to conduct the discussion with a view solely to understanding each other in the hope that understanding may at a later date lead to some measure of agreement.

Ideally in discussion so conducted no one thinks of himself as defending the "truth"; by the "truth" is meant simply whatever all may eventually agree upon. All regard the discussion as a process, not influenced in substance by anyone, out of which consensus *may* grow naturally. And all attempt to take the following attitudes. Toward the discussion as a whole: the only objective is to understand the thinking of others; no one thinks in terms of winning or losing the discussion; no one attempts to influence others or expects to be influenced. Toward the other participants: all equally are regarded as possible sources of what the group may eventually regard as the truth. Toward the views presented in discussion: all views are presumed to contain some of the truth, and no view is regarded as the property of any participant but of the group as a whole.

These pious recommendations can sometimes be translated into reality if the group is willing to follow one special rule in its discussion and under the guidance of the moderator to follow a special pattern. The rule is that, except for the moderator, no one is to make a declarative statement except in reply to a question. When in response to a question a member presents his view for examination, discussion conforms to the following pattern:

1. UNDERSTANDING THE VIEW. If a participant thinks the view is not clear, he may ask questions for clarification. When he believes he understands the view, in response to a question from the moderator or the presenter of the view, he states the view in his own words and asks the one who presented it whether he would accept the statement as accurate; if he will not accept it, the process continues until the questioner can state the view to the satisfaction of the member who presented it. Various members may take the role of questioner, as the view is examined until it is certain that all understand it.

2. EXPLORING THE VIEW WITHOUT PASSING JUDGMENT ON IT. Any participant may then ask questions regarding how the view differs from alternative views or concerning the unexpressed premises or implications of the view. He may also ask questions regarding particular points in connection with the view that he believes the entire group might accept. And he may ask for information regarding possible research that might resolve the difference of opinion regarding the view.

3. CONCLUDING DISCUSSION OF THE VIEW. When consensus apparently exists, the moderator phrases for approval by the group a statement of "the sense of the meeting" on the view. If consensus does not exist, he takes care in summarizing the discussion to do justice to whatever diversity of opinion still exists.

This process is then repeated as other views are presented. At no time during the discussion is argument permitted; the only objective of the discussion is to achieve understanding. Such understanding may or may not lead eventually to agreement, but in difficult situations it is at any rate a first indispensable step toward agreement. Experience indicates that with some training and experience both moderator and participants can follow the procedure rather closely. In difficult situations it is worth trying.

References

Dewey, John, *How We Think*, Boston: D. C. Heath & Company, 1933.

Gulley, Halbert E., *Discussion, Conference, and Group Process*, New York: Holt, Rinehart and Winston, Inc., 1960, Chap. 10.

Keltner, John W., "Goals, Obstacles, and Problem Formulation in Group Discussion," *The Quarterly Journal of Speech*, December, 1947, p. 468.

Leigh, Robert D., *Group Leadership*, New York: W. W. Norton & Company, Inc., 1936, Chap. 2.

McBurney, James E. and Kenneth G. Hance, *Discussion in Human Affairs*, New York: Harper & Row, Publishers, 1950, Chap. 6.

Osborn, Alex F., *Applied Imagination*, New York: Charles Scribner's Sons, 1961.

Rapoport, Anatol, *Fights, Games, and Debates*, Ann Arbor: University of Michigan Press, 1960, p. 245 ff.

Sattler, William M. and N. Edd Miller, *Discussion and Conference*, Englewood Cliffs, N.J.: Prentice-Hall, Inc., 1954, Chap. 7.

Wagner, Russell H. and Carroll C. Arnold, *Handbook of Group Discussion*, Boston: Houghton Mifflin Company, 1950, Chap. 5.

CHAPTER 5

Participating in Discussion

Determining a pattern to follow and following it are activities of the group as a whole, and we have discussed them without specific reference to the individual. But the success of group thinking obviously depends very much upon how effectively the members contribute and how skillfully the leader moderates the discussion. In this and the following chapter we shall look at group discussion from the point of view first of the participant and then of the moderator.

That some people are more useful members of a committee or round table than others is too obvious to need emphasis. Anyone who has often served on committees will testify that some few persons are invaluable at the conference table. Others contribute little, while still others are positive nuisances.

To the question, What makes a good committee member? there are of course many answers. Knowledge of the matter under discussion, a quick mind, sound judgment, and verbal facility are all important. The first can be acquired by anyone who will take the trouble to inform himself, and any participant in discussion should be willing to make this effort. There is little one can do about the second except to cultivate a habit of mental alertness, while soundness of judgment and skill in expression are the result of experience and long practice. If we confine our attention to those matters on which rapid improvement is possible, we shall find that a committee member's value depends primarily on his attitudes, on what may be called his discussion habits, and on his ability to perform certain functions in discussion.

Attitudes

1. FRIENDLINESS. The close cooperation required in group thinking occurs only in an atmosphere of good will. It follows that each member's attitude toward his colleagues should be one of friendliness and courtesy. We do not open our minds freely unless we feel that we are among friends, and stiffness, formality, or pomposity chills the atmosphere and freezes discussion. Still more destructive of congeniality is open hostility or loss of temper; either makes fruitful discussion impossible. The committee member needs the imperturbable good humor and unfailing courtesy of the trained diplomat.

2. OPEN-MINDEDNESS. Toward the ideas presented in discussion the desirable attitude is open-mindedness. Often the member will have an opinion on the question before the discussion starts, and it is not to be expected that he will check his opinion at the door on entering the committee room. Nor need he feel that he cannot defend his opinion earnestly and forthrightly; frankness is necessary to profitable discussion. At the same time no cooperative thinking is possible if the question is closed in the minds of some members before discussion starts. We should hold our opinions tentatively and be willing to reopen a question, giving sympathetic consideration to any new light that may be thrown on it.

So far as is humanly possible our attitude in discussion should be that of the inquirer rather than of the advocate. When the group quickly polarizes into two debate teams, each committed in advance to a particular conclusion and bent on bearing the other down by the weight of numbers or argument, little group thinking can take place. Each member should feel that what he says is off the record, that sticking to one's guns in spite of the evidence is a fault rather than a virtue, and that the only man who never changes his mind is the one who never thinks.

3. INDEPENDENCE OF MIND. To extol the virtues of open-mindedness does not mean, however, that one should abandon his independence of mind. There is abundant evidence, based on both observation and experimentation, that many persons find it extremely difficult to resist majority pressure, whether the majority is right or wrong—and the majority is frequently wrong. When in a minority one should listen sympathetically to what the majority is saying and weigh their arguments carefully but should not change his mind unless really convinced that he was wrong; "me too" voices in discussion are not useful. And of course the majority also should take care not to coerce minority members or to discourage their participation; too often it turns out that they were right.

4. INTEREST. Toward the discussion as a whole the member's attitude should be one of lively and sympathetic interest. And he should show his interest. The fishy eye, the poker face, the wooden voice, and the distant manner are enemies of good discussion. It should be apparent to our colleagues that we are keenly interested in the problem before them and wish to cooperate actively in the search for a solution satisfactory to the entire group.

We sometimes speak of a certain person as having an ideal personality for committee work. But do we mean anything more than that he is friendly and courteous toward other members of the group, that he is hospitable to new ideas, that he maintains his independence of mind, and that he displays keen interest in the business before the committee? We need not surrender too easily to the mystery of personality. The attitudes that make for effective participation can be developed by nearly anyone who is willing to take himself in hand.

We have discussed four attitudes favorable to effective participation. One might of course list also attitudes unfavorable to good participation. Among such attitudes are those of the blocker, who is almost habitually against any suggestion made; the dominator, who attempts to force his views on others, perhaps trying to do most of the talking; the special-interest pleader, who has a private ax to grind and will not look at the problem objectively; the play-boy, who refuses to take the discussion seriously; the recognition seeker, who insists upon a privileged status for himself; the cynic, who questions the motives of other participants and doubts the value of every idea presented; and the uncritical follower, already noted above, who agrees with whatever is being said without weighing argument. It is useful to consider whether one may habitually be playing one of these obstructive roles in discussion.[1]

Discussion Habits

Certain habits of thought and speech are favorable to good discussion. Not all possess these habits, but practically anyone can acquire them if he understands what they are and is willing to discipline himself in discussion. Among the more important are those suggested below.

1. SPEAK UP! Cooperative thinking is possible only when mind reacts to mind—and mind reading is a lost art. The member of the group must, so to speak, think aloud so that others may know what is going on in his mind. It is a mistake to suppose that he should speak only when he has a new idea or argument to present. He should speak also to let the group know how he is reacting to the ideas and arguments presented by others. If he speaks infrequently or only when called upon by the chairman, he slows up the discussion. General and lively participation facilitates group thinking.

2. DON'T INTERRUPT! The suggestion that one should participate freely does not mean that he should interrupt others. When two are talking at the same time, nothing useful is happening, and the person with a low emotional boiling point who constantly inter-

---

[1] For a fuller discussion of these attitudes see Waldo H. Braden and Earnest Brandenburg, *Oral Decision-Making*, New York: Harper & Row, Publishers, 1955, Chap. 13.

rupts may easily become a nuisance. If the idea the member wishes to express is worth presenting at all, a delay of a few seconds will not detract from its value.

3. FOLLOW THE BALL! Effective participation is not merely self-expression; it involves bridling the impulse to give voice immediately to whatever idea comes to mind without regard to whether it will advance the discussion. The desire merely to get something off one's chest must be curbed if discussion is to make any progress.

The thoughtful member of a discussion group keeps his eye on the agenda and remembers what issue is at the moment under discussion; he listens carefully to what others are saying and makes the effort necessary to understand them; and when he speaks, he speaks to the point. During the exploratory phase of discussion of an issue, he sticks to that issue, expressing his own view on it or commenting on the views that have been expressed by others. When the group is attempting to resolve a conflict of opinion, his contribution usually expresses his reaction to what the last speaker has said. In this phase discussion is much like a game of tennis; the speaker should return the ball that comes over the net toward him, not some other ball he has been hiding in his pocket. To keep his bearings during discussion the participant may find it useful to take notes of the kind suggested for the moderator in the next chapter.

4. BE BRIEF! Typically discussion takes the form of conversation rather than of an exchange of long statements. Seldom should a contribution be more than a few sentences in length, and often a few words are sufficient. The long contributions that slow up progress are sometimes due to sheer verbosity; many words are used to say what could have been said more clearly in a few. Terseness is a virtue, for unnecessary words usually cloud the point. Or the unduly long contribution may result from the speaker's attempt to present a series of points. Usually one point only should be presented in each contribution; if several are presented at the same time, the attempt on the part of the group

to discuss all of them together breeds confusion. The member who insists on presenting several points in the same contribution often is an experienced public speaker suffering from a common occupational disease of the orator—the inability to break up what he has to say into the small units appropriate for discussion. Be brief, then, in the sense of presenting one point at a time and of expressing that point as tersely as possible.

5. AVOID NAME-CALLING! Some persons have a habit of so expressing themselves as to arouse hostility or opposition which the idea expressed would not itself have encountered. They refer to liberals, for example, as "pinks" or to conservatives as "reactionaries" or "fascists." In discussion we should avoid all name-calling words and other language tinged with emotion; it is likely to set off a chain reaction of recrimination that will make the subject too hot to handle. The use of such language may spring from an attitude of hostility, but often it is only a verbal habit of which the user is quite unaware. In discussion we may speak frankly and earnestly, but so far as possible we should use language that does not arouse unnecessary opposition to the ideas expressed.

The Tasks of the Participant

Apart from the attitudes and habits of the participant, it is useful to consider what functions he will find it useful to perform in discussion. He has three principal obligations: to do his part in helping to develop and maintain a climate favorable to good discussion, to encourage good orientation of the group's thinking, and to make contributions to the substance of the discussion. He can often help to create a favorable climate by expressing good will toward the other members, by complimenting others on their contributions, by encouraging others to speak, and by helping to pacify the short-tempered and to harmonize divergent views. He can sometimes encourage well-oriented thinking by asking for or providing orientation, by asking for or providing procedural suggestions, by asking for or making summary statements. And of course he can contribute to the substance of the discussion by asking for or contributing information, by asking for a statement of opinion or by stating his own opinion, by elaborating his own argument or asking another to elaborate his argument, by asking for critical comment or by offering critical comment on a view presented, by asking for or offering clarification, and by agreeing or disagreeing with a view presented. Anyone making such contributions is a useful member of a group.

References

Braden, Waldo W. and Earnest Brandenburg, *Oral Decision-Making,* New York: Harper & Row, Publishers, 1955, Chaps. 2, 12, 13.

Chase, Stuart, *Roads To Agreement,* New York: Harper & Row, Publishers, 1951, Chap. 6.

Gulley, Halbert E., *Discussion, Conference, and Group Process,* New York: Holt, Rinehart and Winston, Inc., 1960, Chaps. 5, 6.

Sattler, William M. and N. Edd Miller, *Discussion and Conference,* Englewood Cliffs, N.J.: Prentice-Hall, Inc., 1954, Chap. 14.

CHAPTER 6

Moderating Discussion

No orchestra attempts to play a symphony without a conductor to coordinate and direct its efforts. Nor does a discussion group, if it is wise, attempt to solve a problem without a moderator to guide its thinking. Though the leader usually makes no contribution to the substance of the argument, his services as coordinator and director are essential to group thinking.

The importance of the moderator arises from the fact that in group thinking several minds are cooperating in a joint enterprise. To act together and to react upon each other the minds must think aloud. This immediately creates a traffic problem. If each member speaks as the spirit moves him, some will speak often, others not at all; or several will talk at the same time. And an arrangement by which each takes his turn in rotation is much too mechanical for the informal give and take of group thinking. What is needed is a traffic officer who stands outside of the argument but follows it closely enough to see who should have the floor next.

Difficulty will arise also from the desire of each member to discuss whatever point happens to interest him most at the moment. With each member hot upon the trail of his own idea, the attention of the group will seldom remain focused long on any one point unless someone makes it his business to direct attention to that point. And unless discussion can be focused on one point at a time, no progress toward a conclusion is possible.

There is need, too, for someone not a party to the argument to keep an eye on the developing situation as a whole, for each member of the group is too intent on the point he is making or criticizing to keep the total picture in view. Of necessity he takes a worm's-eye rather than a bird's-eye view of the scene. Without a leader the group soon loses its sense of direction; and even when it sticks to a point long enough to explore it thoroughly, the group is often at a loss to know "where we go from here."

Dependence of the group on a moderator argues no lack of mental capacity on the part of its members. The need arises from the nature of group thinking itself. Several minds cannot cooperate effectively in discussion without someone to coordinate their efforts, and failure is almost assured when the group does not realize that it needs a moderator or when the moderator does not understand his function.

To moderate discussion well is an exacting task, requiring mental alertness, emotional maturity, and a sense of method. But the necessary attitudes are neither mysterious nor rare, and the method can be learned. In the following pages attention will be directed to the problem of preparing to lead, to some of the attitudes desirable in a discussion leader's personality, and to specific functions the leader must perform if group thinking is to be profitable.

Preparing for the Discussion

While all members of the group should feel a responsibility to prepare themselves for the discussion, preparation is especially necessary for the moderator. In addition to being as well informed as possible on the problem to be discussed, he should feel a special responsibility for making the preliminary arrangements. His first task often is to make sure that the necessary information will be available to the group. As we have noted in Chapter 2, this may be done in one or more of four ways: all members of the group may be requested in advance to inform themselves and advised where they can find information, several members of the group may be appointed to inform themselves on particular aspects of the problem and to make short informative statements before discussion is attempted, special resource persons may be invited to attend, or the moderator himself may prepare to serve as a resource person. Whatever method is employed, it usually is the responsibility of the moderator to see that proper provision has been made.

If the moderator foresees that visual aids will be useful, he should see to it that they are properly prepared and so displayed that all can see them. Such aids may take the form of maps, charts, diagrams, or graphs. They should be as simple and intelligible as possible and prepared with such care that no one can question their accuracy or fail to understand them.

The moderator should also give a good deal of thought to the agenda that he believes the group will find it useful to follow and if possible should have a suggested agenda on a blackboard where all can see it. He should not, however, impose his agenda on the group against its will. Rather he should suggest the desirability of following an agenda, propose one for the group's consideration, and after inviting comment from the group make such changes as may be desired. Usually, if he has given careful thought to the agenda, the group will be glad to accept it with few changes.

Finally, it is usually the moderator's responsibility to insure that the physical arrangements are as satisfactory as possible. He should especially consider the seating arrangement and such matters as lighting, heat, and ventilation. Unless members of the group are comfortable, discussion will suffer.

Conducting the Session

THE MODERATOR'S PERSONALITY. The good discussion leader is a genial, friendly person, courteous and considerate to the members of his group and genuinely interested in them as persons. Regarding them as his guests, he tries to make each feel that he is among friends and that whatever he contributes is valued. For it is the leader's special responsibility to create and maintain the atmosphere of good will essential to group thinking. To succeed not only must he himself be a person of good will; he must possess the patience and tact to allay the ill will sometimes created by others. No matter how annoying a member may be, the leader must remain imperturbably good-humored if he is to keep conversation on the level where profitable exchange of ideas is possible.

But the effective leader is interested not only in the members of his group as persons; he is interested also in the question discussed, in the ideas and suggestions presented, and in the orderly progress of the discussion toward a conclusion. And he shows his interest. If an apathetic group member handicaps the discussion, an apathetic leader is likely to kill it. The leader's face, voice, and manner should suggest keen interest in the discussion and genuine concern that it make progress. Enthusiasm is contagious, and the leader should have an inexhaustible supply of it.

Toward the ideas presented in discussion the leader's attitude should be one of strict impartiality. He cannot afford to compromise his position as moderator by becoming a party to the argument. Usually he should even avoid revealing what his own opinion is on the question under discussion. To take sides in the argument is to vacate the moderator's chair, and the group cannot function effectively without its moderator. The leader is performing a professional service for the group in assisting it to explore the problem thoroughly and to think its way through to a conclusion that its members find satisfactory. Whether he personally approves of the conclusion is immaterial.

Insistence upon the moderator's impartiality does not imply, however, that he cannot call the attention of the group to facts it is overlooking. Nor does it imply that he cannot invite consideration of argument being ignored. He may say, for example, "You seem agreed on this point, but what would you say to those who argue this way?" and he states the point that he feels should be examined. He takes care not to present it as his own or to criticize the group for rejecting it. If they examine the point fairly, he is satisfied.

Finally, an attitude of responsibility is characteristic of the good discussion leader. This may seem to have been implied in what has already been said, but the point will bear emphasizing.

Too many moderators apparently feel that their only task is to keep the discussion going. When a lively exchange is in progress they settle back to take a rest until the discussion threatens to stall. This will hardly do. The leader must help the group think its problem through. As will appear later in this chapter, he has many functions to perform. To perform them well he must follow every turn of the argument with the closest attention, ready to step in immediately when his assistance is required. Make no mistake about it, moderating discussion well is exacting work.

So far as personality is concerned, then, the genial, interested, impartial, and responsible person is the one most likely to succeed as a discussion leader.

THE MODERATOR'S FUNCTIONS. It is of course possible to possess the attitudes favorable to good leadership and yet know little of the leader's duties. That he has specific functions to perform in the process of group thinking is verified daily in the observation and experience of those who conduct much business at the conference table. It is somewhat difficult to discuss the leader's functions in sufficient detail to be helpful without making them seem mechanical. Alert and sensitive adaptation to the shifting situation is always required. But beneath the adaptation and improvisation one can usually see the experienced leader doing certain things essential to the success of the discussion. In the following paragraphs five specific functions of the moderator will be suggested.

Regulating the discussion. The moderator's most elementary function is to regulate the discussion in such a way that all members have an equal opportunity to participate. He is, in short, a traffic officer. In practice, to discharge this function well is not so simple as it sounds.

Nearly every group has one or two members who talk too often, too long, or at the wrong time. Some of them are people with low emotional boiling points who break into speech on slight provocation. The impatient member may have the annoying habit of interrupting others. When such interruptions occur frequently, they try the patience of other members and embarrass discussion.

If the member who is interrupted stops talking, he is likely to feel annoyed; if he does not stop talking, the resulting confusion wastes time. Or the offending member, though he does not interrupt, may speak so frequently that soon he is monopolizing the conversation. Confronted with problems of this kind, the leader may find it necessary to ask members to raise their hands when they wish to speak. He will then recognize first those who have talked least often, unless at the time there is some special reason why one member should do more than his share of the talking. Most leaders would prefer to avoid even this slight formality, but it is less objectionable than allowing a few members to monopolize the conversation or to interrupt constantly.

Another troublesome member is the one who cannot say anything in less than ten minutes and would prefer half an hour. Often he is having difficulty in expressing himself. After stating his point he feels he has not made it clear, so he states it again and still again. By the time he finishes, the point has been lost in a cloud of words. Before allowing discussion to proceed, the leader should restate the point clearly and tersely. To allow the group to react to the contribution without understanding it invites confusion.

Sometimes the speaker's difficulty is that he does not understand the point himself and is thinking aloud as he tries to formulate it. If so, the leader may sharpen the speaker's thinking by putting a question to him. Occasionally the leader, who is usually familiar with the arguments on the subject, grasps the point before the speaker himself does. If so, he may say, "Is this what you mean?" and then state the point himself. In situations of this kind the moderator should assume that the point may be important and should help the speaker in any way that he can. He should never betray impatience at the speaker's inability to make himself clear.

The unduly long contribution is sometimes due not to verbosity or inability to express oneself, but to the desire to present more than one point. The member has a number of related points in mind and would like to present them in a single statement. At times an extended statement may be desirable, but usually discussion will proceed more rapidly if one point is presented at a time, so that the group can comment on it before it has been forgotten. When a speaker has presented a point and is launching into another with the apparent intention of delivering a speech, the leader should interrupt with some such remark as this: "I see that you have more argument to present, but suppose we take it one point at a time, commenting on each point as you go along." He should not fail later to return to the speaker for the rest of his argument.

The private whispered conversations that sometimes spring up must be dealt with lest they split the group into fragments. If the leader interrupts the general discussion, the whispered conversation is usually terminated abruptly. If it is not, the leader may say, "I wonder if all of us shouldn't be in on the point you are making. What is it?" In most cases the private conversation turns out to have been entirely relevant. The offending member had a point to make but was too shy to speak out; so he turned to his neighbor with it. What the leader needs in a situation of this kind is a combination of good-humored firmness and a light touch.

The reticent member also may present a problem. Does he really have nothing to say, or is he only shy? Not much can be done about the member who has nothing to say. In a practical working committee, he contributes nothing and is so much dead weight—though he may be profiting personally. In a community round table there are often a few members who contribute little or nothing but feel that they get a good deal from listening to the others. If there are not too many of them, they do no harm and should not be made to feel unwelcome.

But one should not take it for granted that the less talkative member has nothing to say. When he has overcome his shyness, he may prove to be the best informed and most thoughtful member of the group. Such a person will usually respond to a direct question or to a request for his opinion on the point under discussion. And when he has heard his own voice a few times and feels more at home, he may participate freely enough.

In moderating discussion for a group whose members are unaccustomed to talking in public, it may be necessary to break an initial crust of shyness before any discussion at all can be started.

The leader may go the rounds, asking each in turn to express his opinion. When conflicting opinions have been expressed, he encourages those in disagreement to elaborate their views and reply to each other's arguments. A lively discussion is soon under way. One should not be disturbed if some of the first contributions are irrelevant or unimpressive. The object at the moment is to get any kind of discussion started. It can later be given direction and depth.

Asking individual members for expressions of opinion should never be regarded as more than a device for breaking the ice. Some leaders employ it habitually, so that what should be discussion among members becomes a cross-examination of the group by the leader. The leader should not be satisfied until a lively exchange is going on among the members themselves.

Focusing the discussion. If members of the group supply the ammunition in discussion, it is the leader's job to keep the weapon trained on the target. It is not enough that members stick to the general subject under discussion; their attention must be kept focused on the specific point at that moment under consideration, a much more difficult task. The leader may ignore some irrelevant remarks; often they do not tempt the group from its task. But if others follow the wandering member off into the underbrush, the leader must bring them back. Unless attention can be kept to a specific point under consideration long enough to thresh it out and bring it to a conclusion, no decision can be reached.

The average person's apparent inability to follow discussion and stick to the point may at first astonish and then exasperate the inexperienced leader. "How can Jones fail to see," he may exclaim to himself, "that his contribution has no bearing on the point Brown has just made or on the situation as it stood at the conclusion of Brown's remarks?" Usually the explanation is that Jones simply was not listening to Brown; he was busy deciding what he would say when Brown had finished. The ability to follow the ball in discussion is comparatively rare, and the leader will sometimes feel that he spends most of his time setting discussion back on the track.

A tactful way to check the tendency to wander is to ask the

member whose remark seems irrelevant, "Can you make more clear to us how your point bears on the issue we are now discussing?" If the remark is irrelevant, the member is usually willing to drop it. Often it is relevant to some phase of the problem not then under consideration. If so, the leader should assure the speaker that it will be taken up later, and should take care to return to it at the appropriate time.

How sharply the leader can keep discussion focused on each point as it is considered depends a good deal on the size of the group and on how accustomed its members are to thinking together. The larger the group, the more difficult it will be to keep attention focused, especially if its members are unaccustomed to discussion. Sometimes the leader will feel that the best he can do is to keep discussion to each major subdivision of the problem in turn without attempting to focus attention on each minor issue that comes up. He will learn only by experience how to steer a safe course between letting the discussion run wild and making a pedantic nuisance of himself.

Guiding the discussion. Discussion that is well regulated and focused may still make little progress unless the moderator guides the discussion in several ways. However pertinent and well-informed the discussion is on particular points, the group will not arrive at any destination unless it can maintain a sense of direction, an awareness of the over-all pattern to which its discussion should conform.

Specifically, the group must keep in view the agenda indicating the major issues to be examined. In examining any one of the issues it must usually follow the steps suggested in Chapter 4: exploration of the issue, taking stock of the situation, resolution of the disagreements, and summary. And in threshing out any conflict of opinion, discussion must be directed to the mutual examination and criticism of supporting arguments. Very few groups can keep their bearings in these three respects without the guidance of a leader; each member is too intent upon the point being made at the moment to keep the total picture in mind. It is peculiarly the leader's responsibility to keep the broader picture in mind, to keep his bearings in the welter of detailed discussion, and to provide the group with a sense of direction.

Clarifying the discussion. The individual thinker, however skilled, is in constant danger of lapsing into confusion. His attention wanders; his map of the problem he is exploring wavers before his eyes and fades like a mirage; his ideas lose their sharpness and melt into a confused heap. To make any progress he must repeatedly pull himself up short and redirect his efforts. How much greater is the danger of confusion when several are working together on a problem! But how can a group pull itself up short to clarify its thinking? It cannot. That must be done for it by the moderator. He is, among other things, the clarifier of group thinking.

Need will arise frequently to clarify or interpret a member's contribution to the rest of the group. We have already noted the difficulty a member often has in stating his point clearly. He obscures it in a cloud of words or uses language so inexpertly that his hearers are left in the dark; sometimes he does not understand the point clearly himself. To avoid confusion the leader must step in to rephrase the point, to sharpen the speaker's thinking with a few well-directed questions, or to state the point himself if he believes he understands it better than the speaker does. Not until the point is clear to the group can discussion proceed without danger of confusion.

But obscure contributions are not the only source of confusion in discussion. Frequently the situation itself becomes confused, and members look at each other blankly as someone inquires, "Well, where are we now, anyway?" To this question the moderator should always have the answer. As pilot of the ship he should keep his bearings; he should know where the ship is and in what direction it should now steer.

The group, for example, may have lost track of its agenda or may have lost its bearings in the discussion of a particular issue, though all are clear regarding what issue is under consideration. In the following passage the moderator responds to a typical request for clarification.

Member: I'm becoming a little confused. What are we supposed to be talking about now?

Moderator: The discussion *has* become rather mixed up, hasn't it? You'll remember that in our discussion of whether we favor federal aid to education we were to consider three main issues: Do the states need federal aid? Would the present bill provide the aid needed? And is the bill's provision for allocation of funds sound? We have agreed that aid is needed and that this bill would provide it. In exploring the third issue we found ourselves agreeing that the funds would not be allocated among the states strictly according to need and that we disapprove of this. We were disagreed as to whether white and Negro pupils would benefit equally from the funds and are now trying to reach a conclusion on that point.

Confusion is always likely to arise during the exploratory phase of discussion of an issue, when the group is trying to find out where its members stand. This is especially true if the moderator has too long delayed taking stock of the situation. The leader should know which members have not yet made their stand clear, and if the situation has become confused, he should ask them for an expression of opinion so that he can take stock of the situation and sort out the points of agreement and disagreement.

When two members are threshing out a point of disagreement, the discussion may reach a baffling impasse in which no progress is being made, though no one can quite see why. The following passage illustrates the situation.

Thomas: The trouble with this plan of socialized medicine is that as soon as you adopt it the quality of the doctor's work will suffer.

Walton: What reason do you have for thinking so?

Thomas: Why, under this plan the doctor will receive a fixed income.

Walton: He'll get a fixed income, yes. But how does that prove his work will suffer?

Thomas: It's bound to. Here's the way the bill reads: "Each physician employed under the system will receive—"

Walton (interrupting): I'm not arguing about that. I admit the doctor gets a fixed income.

Obviously this conversation is getting nowhere. The difficulty is that Thomas has stated only a part of his argument. The complete argument would run as follows: The doctor's work will suffer, because a fixed income destroys the incentive to do good work, and under this plan the doctor would have a fixed income. Thomas has left the first of the two supporting statements unexpressed. It is this unexpressed point that Walton apparently wishes to challenge, but since the point was not expressed he cannot see how to reply to the argument. The moderator should step in to clarify the situation.

Moderator (to Thomas): The only reason you give for thinking the doctor's work would suffer is that he would receive a fixed income, but don't you mean to say also that a fixed income would destroy his incentive to do good work?

Thomas: Of course.

Moderator: And I take it, Walton, that it's this last point you object to?

Walton: Yes, I don't believe income is the doctor's chief incentive; he's a professional man, not a businessman.

Moderator: Then it's the importance of the doctor's income as an incentive that we ought to be discussing.

There is perhaps no surer mark of the expert moderator than his ability to unravel a snarl of this kind by directing attention to the unexpressed premises of an argument. To see quickly what those premises are often requires some knowledge of the structure of argument. The service the moderator can render at this point is so important that the next chapter will be devoted to an elementary discussion of the structure of argument.

Pointing up the discussion. A mason does not consider his work finished until he has "pointed it up" by running the point of his trowel along the crevices between the bricks to indent the mortar slightly at the joints. The bricklayer points up masonry to improve its appearance. The moderator points up discussion to achieve clarity.

A discussion should have joints and they should be apparent. The division of the entire discussion into sections, each devoted to one of the major issues in the agenda, should be clear. As each issue is taken up, the moderator should state it clearly in interrogative form. If the discussion is long and involved, he may occasionally restate it. During discussion of the issue he will employ brief summary and transitional remarks to distinguish the different phases of the discussion: exploration of the issue, taking stock of the situation, and resolution of disagreements. When discussion of the issue has been completed, he will sum up the result in a few terse sentences and provide a transition to the next issue. At the close of the session he will make a three- or four-minute summary of the entire discussion. This summary should not be a detailed review of all the arguments presented. It should rather restate the principal issues that have been examined and indicate what conclusions, if any, have been reached.

When discussion is pointed up carefully, there is never any doubt as to what at the moment is under discussion, or as to when discussion of the preceding point was terminated or with what result. At the close of the discussion everyone should be able to recall what issues have been discussed and what conclusions have been reached. The untidiness and apparent futility that sensible people often object to in discussion are due in large part to the moderator's failure to point up the discussion.

Taking Notes

By this time it will have occurred to the reader that if the moderator is to keep discussion focused, to guide and clarify it when necessary, and to point it up, he either will need a phenomenal memory or will be obliged to take notes. Most inexperienced leaders rely on memory during the first session or two and then begin to experiment with methods of note taking.

The leader's first attempt to take notes is usually disappointing. He finds his attention so fully occupied with moderating the discussion that he has little time for anything else. One thing becomes clear at once: He cannot possibly jot down all of the many arguments presented. Fortunately he need not do so. What he needs is a brief record indicating clearly and at a glance what issues have been discussed and with what results. With practice he will find it possible to take notes of this kind without unduly distracting his attention from the discussion. In working out his own method the inexperienced leader may find the following suggestions helpful.

Before the discussion begins, set down the agenda on one or two large sheets of paper, stating each issue interrogatively in the fewest possible words and leaving plenty of space between the statements of the issues. As the group explores one of the issues, jot down in a word or two each of the points on which there is agreement, with a check mark after each to indicate agreement. Set down also a word or two followed by an interrogation point to indicate each of the points of conflict revealed during the exploratory period. All of these entries should be indented somewhat to make clear that the points of agreement and disagreement were brought out in discussion of that particular issue in the agenda. Before the points of agreement and disagreement have been brought out clearly, it may become clear that the major issue should be subdivided. If so, write down with indentation the subordinate issues and proceed with each as suggested above.

As each point of conflict is threshed out, write down after your brief statement of it such words as "yes," "no," or "undecided" to indicate what disposition was made of the point. Similar words may be written after your statement of the main issue when its discussion has been completed. The leader's notes covering the illustrative passage with which this chapter closes would look somewhat as follows:

> 3. Ban Party?
>   Banning un-American?—*No*
>   Don't ban because disagree with party's ideas √
>   Ban if conspiring seize government √
>   Ban if agent foreign power √
>   Is party conspiring to seize government?—*Probably*
>   Is party agent of foreign power?—*Undecided*
>   Banning strengthen or weaken party?

The "No" was of course written after "Banning un-American?" at the close of discussion of that issue.

The leader will find that with practice he can set down notes of this kind quickly and almost without looking at the paper. At any point in the discussion a glance at the paper will indicate what is at the moment under consideration, and at the close of the session the moderator can make a brief summary from his notes, indicating what issues and subordinate points have been considered and what disposition was made of each.

The Moderator at Work

Skill in using the methods suggested in this chapter is acquired best by experience. But observation is also a good teacher, and the following annotated passage may serve to illustrate the use of some of the suggestions made in the preceding pages. The discussion occurred in a high school class in social studies at the last of three sessions devoted to consideration of the question: What should be our policy on Communist activities in the United States? The teacher is acting as moderator.

COMMENT

Teacher: In our two previous sessions we discussed Communist activities in labor unions and in government offices. Our conclusion was that while unions should rid themselves of Communist leadership, we do not favor any law forcing them to do so. And we thought that the loyalty test now being applied to government employees will prevent a dangerous amount of Communist activity in government. We come now to the last question in our agenda: Should the American Communist party be banned? What do you think about it, John?

The leader summarizes the previous discussion and states the issue to be examined next.

John: Certainly it should be banned. We've let the Communists go too far already.

The group explores the issue.

Helen: But if you ban the Communists, the next thing you know someone will want to ban the Democratic party. It's against our principles to ban any political party.

Carl: If you ban the Communists, you'll drive them underground. That would only strengthen them.

John: How could it? They could no longer have candidates or make campaign speeches. That would put a stop to a lot of their propaganda.

Clara: Helen says we shouldn't ban any political party. But is the Communist party really a political party?

Helen: Of course it is. It has a platform and candidates like any other party.

Teacher: It seems to me we have two different questions here: Would it be contrary to American principles to ban the Communist party? Would it be expedient to ban it? Let's take them one at a time. Suppose we consider, first, whether it would violate democratic principles to ban the party.

The leader subdivides the issue and invites exploration of the first of the subordinate issues.

John: I don't see anything un-American in banning an organization that is trying its best to overthrow the American government. Where will democracy be if that happens? And another thing: Why should we let Russia send a lot of spies over here to carry out its orders? And then we say we can't do anything about it because it is a political party!

Carl: Now wait a minute! How do you know the Communist party is planning to seize the government? I doubt it. And how do you know the party takes orders from Moscow? I doubt that too.

Helen: I doubt it, too, but I'd agree that democratic principles wouldn't require us to tolerate an organization that takes orders from Russia or is trying to overthrow the government. I wouldn't call that a real political party.

Teacher: Where do you stand on this, Clara?

Clara: Well, I don't think we should do anything to the Communist party, or to any other party, just because we don't like its ideas. That would certainly be un-American.

John: I'd agree with that ordinarily, but what if its idea is to overthrow the government?

Clara: In that case, yes; or if it takes orders from Russia. But you haven't proved that.

Carl: I think John is taking too much for granted here. Sure, ban the party if it takes orders from Moscow, and ban it if it is really planning to overthrow the government. But how about proof on these points? It's like saying we should send more troops to Germany because the Russians are going to seize the whole country, but how do you know Russia is going to seize all of Germany? I don't think she is.

John: I think there is plenty of proof of it. Isn't she getting up a Russian-controlled German army in her part of Germany?

Teacher: I don't see how Russia's plans in Germany have anything to do with whether it would be un-American to ban the Communist party. What is the connection?

John is not following the ball. The leader recalls discussion to the point at issue.

John: Not much maybe, but Carl brought it up.

Carl: I was just using it as an illustration.

Teacher: All right, let's get back to the point.

Helen: I agree with Clara that we shouldn't ban a party just because we don't like

COMMENT

its ideas. But if it isn't actually a political party on the national ballot, that is a different thing. I don't think we should allow a party to represent a foreign government or try to overthrow our own government.

Carl: I'd agree with that.

Teacher: I think it's clear now about where we stand on the issue. You all seem to agree on these points: That it would be against American principles to ban a party just because we don't agree with its ideas, but that this principle ought not to hold if it can be shown that the party is an agent of a foreign government or is planning to seize our own government by force. And we seem to disagree on two points: Does the American Communist party really plan to overthrow the government by force? Is it really an agent of the Russian government? Let's take these two points one at a time. And let's begin with this one: Does the party really plan to overthrow the government by force?

The leader interrupts discussion to take stock of the situation so that attention can be concentrated on the points of disagreement.

John: I think it does.

Carl: But just because you think so doesn't make it so.

John: How can you think anything else?

The group now attempts to resolve the first disagreement.

Teacher: Suppose, John, you give us one of your reasons for thinking the party has such plans.

John: Well, don't they admit it? For instance, Communists admitted it before the Thomas Investigating Committee.

Carl: But the people giving that testimony were ex-Communists. They had no authority to speak for the party. I'll admit that what they said makes me a little suspicious, but still that's not official.

John and Carl are making no progress in resolving the conflict, and the leader probes for supporting arguments.

John: Well, then, what about the platform of the party in the election when Wallace was a candidate? That ought to be official enough.

Helen: You can't prove anything that way. They were in the Wallace party. I mean, the Communists said they would vote for Wallace, and I suppose they did. At least they didn't vote for a Communist. There was nothing about revolution in the Progressive party.

Teacher: I'm not sure I follow you. Do you mean that the Communists had no platform of their own in that election and that the Progressive party platform, which they supported, contains no reference to revolution?

The leader clarifies and restates an obscure contribution before permitting discussion to continue.

Helen: Yes, that's it.

John: I guess you're right about that. But doesn't the party have a constitution or something?

Clara: Yes, it does, and I read it once. It doesn't say anything definitely about seizing the government by force.

Teacher: Do you agree, then, that so far as its official statements are concerned, there is no proof that the party plans to seize the government by force? (All nod assent.)

The leader points up the discussion.

Helen: But does that settle it? Naturally they wouldn't admit it in official statements.

John: Well, look at what the Communist party has done in other countries when it had a chance. Take Czechoslovakia, for instance, or Yugoslavia, or any of those countries. The Communists take over, and that's the end of freedom and democracy. The Communist party always does that. It's the party line. They don't try it of course until they think they're strong enough. Someday they might be strong enough here. That's the day they are waiting for.

Teacher: To put it in a nutshell, the Communist party here would seize the government if it could, because it has done so in Europe. Is that it?

John has obscured his point in a cloud of words. The leader restates it for him.

John: Yes.

Carl: But there was no shooting when they took over in Czechoslovakia. Is that violent revolution?

Helen: No shooting maybe, but there was certainly a show of force, and the opposition was liquidated right away. I'd call that using force.

Carl: I suppose so. But how do you know the American Communist party would do that?

Clara: You can't know for sure, but I think they probably would.

Carl: Maybe so. It sounds reasonable.

Teacher (glancing around the group): Do the rest of you agree with Carl and Clara? (All nod assent though somewhat reluctantly.) I take it, then, that you think the American Communist party probably does hope someday to seize the government by force though there is no way to prove it positively. Let's look now at the point we postponed a few minutes ago: Is the American Communist party the agent of the Russian government?

The leader summarizes and provides a transition to the next point of disagreement.

John: I think it is. I don't mean that its leaders are Russian spies, but I think they take their orders from Moscow.

Helen: I disagree with that. Why do you think so?

John: Because the party always comes out for whatever Russia would like to have us do—like being against the UN action in the Congo.

Helen: Probably quite a few people are against it.

John: I mean they always follow the party line. Russia was against what we were doing in Greece; so the American Communist party was against it too.

Helen: But I'm against what we were doing in Greece. Am I taking orders from Moscow?

John: And Russia was against the UN holding elections in Korea; so the American Communists were against that.

Teacher: I think, John, that Helen agrees that the American Communist party follows the party line. But doesn't your argument imply also that whoever follows the party line must be taking orders from Moscow?

John: Yes, it does.

Teacher (to Helen): And isn't that the part of his argument you disagree with?

Helen: That's it exactly. I might agree with something Russia is in favor of, but that doesn't mean I'm taking orders. Maybe I just happen to think that way.

Teacher (to John): Why do you feel that following the party line necessarily means the party is taking orders from Moscow?

John: You can't prove it, I suppose. But when they *always agree with Russia,* the way the American Communists do, it looks pretty suspicious to me.

Clara: I don't think it does. Communists all over the world tend to think alike. They all have the same Marxist ideas. You'd expect them to agree on particular issues, wouldn't you?

John and Helen are arguing at cross purposes. The leader clarifies the situation by stating the unexpressed premise of John's argument and directing discussion to that premise, the real source of the disagreement.

The leader probes for supporting reasons.

Carl: They'd probably think a good deal alike, but the American Communists sometimes change their position overnight exactly when Russia does. Does that sound plausible if they're not taking orders?

Helen: You may think it isn't plausible, but does that *prove* anything?

Teacher: I expect we'll have to agree to disagree on this point! I know of no way to prove that the American Communist party does, or does not, actually take orders from the Russian government.

As no further progress seems possible, the leader summarizes discussion of the entire issue and proceeds to the next question in the agenda.

Suppose I sum up our discussion so far. You will remember that we agreed to subdivide the issue on banning the Communist party as follows: Would banning it violate democratic principles? Would banning it be inexpedient? On the first of these subordinate issues you agree that our principles would not allow us to ban a party merely because we don't approve of its ideas, but that it would be proper to ban it if it could be shown that the party plans to seize the government by force or is the agent of a foreign government. You cannot agree as to whether the Communist party is the agent of the Russian government or not, but you do agree that the party probably would seize the government if it had a chance. Apparently, then, you would not object to banning the party on principle. But this leaves open our second subordinate issue: Would it be expedient to ban the party? That is, would it strengthen or weaken Communist activities? Let's discuss that now.

References

Braden, Waldo W. and Earnest Brandenburg, *Oral Decision-Making,* New York: Harper & Row, Publishers, 1955, Chap. 11.

Gordon, Thomas, *Group-Centered Leadership,* Boston: Houghton Mifflin Company, 1955.

Gulley, Halbert E., *Discussion, Conference, and Group Process,* New York: Holt, Rinehart and Winston, Inc., 1960, Chaps. 12, 13, 14.

Haiman, Franklyn E., *Group Leadership and Democratic Action,* Boston: Houghton Mifflin Company, 1951.

Sattler, William M. and N. Edd Miller, *Discussion and Conference,* Englewood Cliffs, N.J.: Prentice-Hall, Inc., 1954, Chaps. 9, 10, 11.

Wagner, Russell H. and Carroll C. Arnold, *Handbook of Group Discussion,* Boston: Houghton Mifflin Company, 1950, Chap. 6.

PART TWO

THINKING STRAIGHT

CHAPTER 7

Beneath the Surface
of Argument

"Theirs not to reason why, theirs but to do or die" was spoken of soldiers in battle, not of persons seated at the conference table. It is peculiarly the business of a discussion group "to reason why," for in no other way can a conflict of opinion be resolved. As a group threshes out a disagreement, the conversation typically follows this pattern:

A: I think. . . .
B: Why do you think so?
A: Because. . . .
B: My objection to that reason is. . . .

This presentation and mutual criticism of reasons is the heart of the discussion method when the purpose is to resolve differences of opinion, and the skill with which the conversation is conducted largely determines whether a consensus can be reached.

It is possible to present an argument or criticize another's argument without any technical knowledge of logic. We all do it every day, and clearheaded persons do it well. Yet some knowledge of the structure of argument is useful both to the participant and to the moderator. It enables both to look beneath the surface of discussion to the unexpressed premises of the argument, to grasp the argument more quickly, and to criticize it more sharply.

When a member of a discussion group asserts that veterans

make better-than-average grades in college and is challenged to give a reason for this assertion, he may say that veterans are more mature than average students and would therefore be expected to do better work; he may say that he has examined the records of three hundred typical veteran students and found their average grade to be higher than that of three hundred typical non-veterans; or he may say that Professor Jones, who teaches both kinds of students, testifies that the veterans receive higher grades. The three arguments illustrate respectively the appeal to principle, the appeal to fact, and the appeal to authority.

All three types of argument are legitimate; all may be sound and convincing. But in a particular instance any one of them may be weak or unsound. To know something of the structure of each type and to understand in what ways it is most likely to be weak or fallacious sharpens one's ability both to present and to criticize argument.

The Appeal to Principle

The argument from principle cited above, if expressed completely and in briefed form, would run as follows:

I. Veterans in college receive higher grades than nonveteran students, for
  A. The more mature students receive the higher grades, and
  B. Veterans are more mature than nonveteran students.

Such a unit of argument, called a syllogism, consists of three statements: the conclusion, or point being proved, and two supporting statements, or "reasons," offered as proof. Each of the three points is expressed in a terse but complete declarative sentence; mere phrases (the higher grades of veterans, more mature students, greater maturity of veterans, for example) would not express the points clearly. In other words, one cannot argue without verbs; to state any point in argument clearly requires a complete sentence, expressed or understood.

Observe also that the first supporting point (A) is a general statement, or principle, and that the second (B) is a statement of fact which has the effect of classifying veterans under the general principle presented in the first statement. This is typical of all argument of this kind. In the following examples, chosen at random from discussion and cast into the briefed form, the more general statement appears as the first supporting point, though the order in which the two premises are presented is immaterial so far as the soundness of the argument is concerned.

I. The American Communist party should be banned, for
    A. Any organization seeking to overthrow the government by force should be banned, and
    B. The American Communist party seeks to overthrow the government by force.
I. Banning the Communist party would be un-American, for
    A. Depriving any group of the right of political association is un-American, and
    B. Banning the Communist party would deprive its members of the right of political association.
I. The European Common Market will discourage Communist activity in Europe, for
    A. Economic prosperity discourages Communist activity, and
    B. The European Common Market will promote prosperity in Europe.

While we have these examples of argument from principle before us, we may note that the soundness of such argument depends upon the acceptability of the two supporting statements. Regarding the general principle employed we may always inquire: Is this principle sound? If generally sound, is it universally so or must exceptions sometimes be made to it, and is this case such an exception? Regarding the statement of fact we may inquire: Is this statement true? As a matter of fact objection can be raised to all three of the arguments cited above. In the case of the first argument, for example, it may be doubted by some whether the banning of any organization seeking to overthrow the government is a sound principle which must invariably be acted upon. It may be doubted also whether the American Communist party actually seeks to overthrow the government by force. In other words, some persons would demand further argument in support of the two supporting points.

When we observe the use of this type of argument in ordinary discussion, we are struck immediately by the fact that more often than not the speaker does not state both of the supporting points. He omits either the statement of principle or the statement of fact. Thus when challenged to give his reason for the assertion that the Communist party should be banned, the speaker is likely to say, "I think so because we should ban any organization that is trying to overthrow the government by force"; or he may say, "I think so because the Communist party is trying to overthrow the government by force." The missing point—the "implied premise," as the logicians call it—is of course just as much a part of the argument as the point which is stated. The two points together make up the complete argument, and if the unexpressed point is unsound, the whole argument is unsound.

It is not at all incorrect to omit one of the two supporting statements in an argument appealing to principle; often it seems unnecessary to state both. Yet when a group attempts to resolve a conflict of opinion, confusion often arises because one of the two statements has been omitted. Suppose that Mr. A has been challenged to say why he believes economic aid to Europe will lower our standard of living. He replies: "It will do so because inflation lowers the standard of living." Mr. B, who does not believe the plan will lower the standard of living, is at a loss to know how to reply because he agrees that inflation does lower the standard of living. He cannot see that his objection is to the omitted point in Mr. A's argument, that economic aid to Europe will cause inflation.

If Mr. B had understood the structure of this type of argument, he would immediately have detected the unexpressed premise of the argument and presented his objection to it. And the moderator could have performed a valuable service by stepping into the discussion at this point to supply the missing part of Mr. A's argument, thus bringing the conflict into the open. The ability to make this kind of contribution is one mark of the expert discussion leader. (In this connection read again that portion of Chapter 6 dealing with the moderator's role as clarifier of discussion.)

The tendency to omit one of the premises in argument appealing to principle and the confusion that sometimes results are not the only facts that strike one when observing a discussion group at work. One observes also that the simple units of this type of argument are often combined in an elaborate argument which would fill several pages if written out as an editorial or magazine article; though when two members of a group are threshing out a disputed point, the complete argument is usually presented and criticized one step at a time. For example, a member challenged to support the assertion that the American Communist party should be banned may in the course of a 10-minute discussion present piecemeal an argument which could be briefed as follows, the parentheses indicating unexpressed premises:

I. The Communist party should be banned, for
    A. (Any organization seeking to overthrow the government by force should be banned), and
    B. The Communist party seeks to overthrow the government by force;
    C. (Any organization acting secretly as an agency of a foreign power should be banned); and
    D. The Communist party acts secretly as an agency of a foreign power.

In this argument two coordinate units of reasoning, each composed of a general principle and a statement of fact, are used to support the same conclusion; though since the speaker left the two statements of principle (A and C) unexpressed, he probably would say that he had given two reasons only for banning the Communist party.

Several units of argument may also be combined in another way: one unit may be used to support a supporting statement of another unit, as is done twice in the following example:

I. The Communist party should be banned, for
    A. Any organization seeking to overthrow the government by force should be banned, and
    B. The Communist party seeks to overthrow the government by force, for
        1. Any party committed to a philosophy of revolution will seek to overthrow the government by force, and

2. The Communist party is committed to a philosophy of revolution, for
   (a) The philosophy of Marx as interpreted by Lenin is a philosophy of revolution, and
   (b) The American Communist party is committed to the Marx–Lenin philosophy.

In actual discussion this argument probably would be presented one unit at a time. Let us suppose Jones has asserted that the Communist party should be banned. When asked by Smith for his reason, he replies with points (A) and (B). Smith accepts (A) but challenges the truth of (B), and Jones supports (B) with points (1) and (2). Again Smith accepts the first point and challenges the second, and Jones presents (a) and (b) in support of (2). This process may continue for some time as Smith digs deeper and deeper toward the roots of Jones's thinking. Eventually Jones will arrive at premises which Smith must accept, or Jones will confess his inability to carry the argument further. In the former case, agreement has been reached; in the latter also agreement has been reached if Jones now abandons his conclusion. He may of course abandon this particular line of argument and attempt to support his conclusion in some other way. In either case both men have done some real thinking, and their difference of opinion has been clarified.

It is also possible that when one of Jones's premises has been challenged, he will continue to insist on its truth though unable to produce any argument to support it. This will occur most often when the premise is a disputed statement of fact. Unless the statement can be verified, no further progress is possible, and discussion of the point should be postponed pending further investigation. When verification is impossible, the discussion may still have been worth while, for the area of disagreement separating the two men has been much reduced.

The following fragment of discussion may serve to illustrate some of the observations on argument from principle made in the preceding pages.

Moderator: Our difference of opinion here is over whether or not some form of national health insurance would be desirable. How do you feel about it, Steiner?

Steiner: I am definitely of the opinion that it would be undesirable.

Mack: Would you mind telling us why you think so?

Steiner: Not at all. I have two reasons for objecting to such a proposal. The first has to do with the relationship between physician and patient. It seems to me highly desirable that the patient be free to choose his own physician.

Mack: I quite agree. But why do you assume that he couldn't choose his own physician under national health insurance?

Steiner: Well, could he?

Mack: He certainly could under the proposed plan. The patient is free to go to any physician in his community who is associated with the system.

Steiner: In that case I wouldn't object, or at any rate I wouldn't raise this particular objection. I would still object to government health insurance on other grounds.

Mack: What other grounds?

Steiner: On the ground that such a plan would be ineffective; that is, that actually it would not make medical services available to many people.

Mack: Why not?

Steiner: Because you'd have to have the cooperation of the medical profession. I'm assuming here that under the plan you have in mind the physician would not be compelled to enter the system.

Mack: That's right, and it does mean that to be effective the system would need the support and cooperation of a large proportion of the medical men of the country.

Steiner: Well, I just do not believe that any considerable number would be willing to serve under the system.

Mack: I'm more optimistic than you are on that score.

Steiner: You very well know that the American Medical Association is opposed to any such plan. It has taken an official stand against government health insurance plans.

Mack: I understand it has, but that doesn't convince me that doctors would refuse to join the system.

Steiner: The association, through its official spokesmen, has repeatedly put itself on record as opposed to it.

Moderator (to Steiner): I gather that Mack does not question the fact that the American Medical Association disapproves of government health insurance. But your argument also assumes, does it not, that the great majority of medical men will follow the lead of the AMA in this matter?

Steiner: Yes.

Moderator (to Mack): And isn't that where you part company with Steiner?

Mack: Yes, I am not at all convinced that the AMA expresses the views of the medical profession as a whole on this question, nor do I think the average physician will be deterred from joining the plan just because the AMA opposes it. (To Steiner) Have you any evidence that the AMA can speak for the entire medical profession on this question?

Steiner: No, no actual evidence, but personally I have no doubt that it does.

Moderator: I doubt if further discussion on this point would serve any purpose unless one of you can produce evidence on it.

The entire argument presented by Steiner in the course of this conversation might be briefed as follows:

I. Adoption of a plan of national health insurance would be undesirable, for
    A. The patient should be free to choose his own physician, and
    B. Under national health insurance the patient would be assigned arbitrarily to a physician;
    C. Any ineffective plan is undesirable, and
    D. National health insurance would be ineffective, for
        1. It cannot be effective without the cooperation of most of the physicians, and
        2. Most physicians would refuse to join it, for
            a. They will not join a system opposed by the American Medical Association, and
            b. The American Medical Association opposes national health insurance.

A comparison of the outlined argument and the actual discussion makes it clear that in his original presentation of the argument Steiner omitted premises (IB), (IC), and (ID2a). Only the last omission caused difficulty requiring the intervention of the moderator. The net result of the entire discussion was to reduce the original head-on disagreement over the desirability of national health insurance to a disagreement over the single question whether the medical profession generally would follow the American Medical Association in its opposition to the plan.

Considerable space has been given here to the discussion of argument from principle because probably four-fifths of all argument presented in discussion is of this type. But the appeal to fact and the appeal to authority must also be considered.

The Appeal to Fact

In supporting an assertion challenged in discussion one may appeal to fact through the use of *generalization* or *analogy*.

GENERALIZATION. This form of argument attempts to establish the truth of a general statement by citing specific instances in support of it, as when one tries to prove that veterans receive high grades in college by citing the example of a number of veterans who have received such grades. Most of us are probably too easily impressed by argument of this sort. Certainly we should attach very little weight to a generalization based on a handful of instances, as in the argument that the closed shop restricts output because it is known to have done so in a dozen cases. It probably would be easy to find a dozen cases in which the closed shop has not restricted output.

Usually the number of instances required for a sound generalization runs into the hundreds or thousands, and the argument becomes essentially statistical in character. The Gallup Public Opinion Poll is a familiar example of generalization of this kind. The result of the poll is a general statement regarding what the majority of voters will do on election day based on a study of how some thousands of them have said they would vote. The compilation and interpretation of such statistical data is highly technical work requiring professional training and is subject to error even when done by experts.

In evaluating argument of this kind the laymen will do well to raise the following questions:

1. Was the study on which the generalization was based conducted by persons qualified for it by training and experience?
2. Was the study based on a sufficient number of instances?
3. What assurance is there that the instances chosen were typical?
4. In drawing conclusions were the data correctly interpreted?

No one of these questions admits of an easy answer. How many instances, for example, are necessary for a sound generalization? Much depends on the nature of the question being investigated. In the exact sciences a few instances, or even a single instance, might be sufficient. When a physicist conducts an experiment to determine at what temperature chemically pure water will boil under a given atmospheric pressure, he can control all of the factors likely to affect the result. Theoretically one carefully conducted experiment might warrant a conclusion. The situation in the social sciences is very different. There the factors which may affect the result of an investigation are so many and so difficult to identify and isolate that a large number of instances must be examined.

How many instances the social scientist must examine to warrant a conclusion depends in part on what assurance he has that the instances chosen are typical of the class from which they are drawn. And this in turn depends upon his method of selecting the instances. He may select them at random; for example, in conducting a questionnaire study of popular reaction to a radio program the investigator may select every tenth name appearing in the telephone directory. He assumes that under this method the atypical instances will cancel each other and not materially affect the result. But can he be sure that telephone users as a class are typical of those who listen to the radio? Perhaps not. He may then decide to follow a method of weighted sampling, as is done in conducting a public opinion poll. This involves identifying the factors which may affect the result, such as income level and geographical location. The investigator then determines what proportion of the total population falls within each group and draws a corresponding proportion of his instances from each of those groups.

Even when an investigation has been competently conducted, it is possible to misinterpret the results, as when confident predictions regarding the presidential election of 1948 were based on public-opinion polls. The Gallup poll indicated that when the investigation was concluded a few weeks before the election, a majority of the voters intended to support Governor Dewey. Apparently many changed their minds during the closing days of the campaign.

ANALOGY. This form of argument also appeals to fact but is based on the similarity between two institutions or situations. One might argue, for example, that a world federal government would preserve peace among nations because the government of the United States has, with one exception, preserved peace among the states. The soundness of the argument depends upon the closeness of the analogy. Is the problem of preserving peace among the nations essentially like that of preserving peace among our own states? Clearly the two situations have a good deal in common but are they alike in regard to those conditions that affect the preservation of peace? This is not an easy question to answer. To evaluate the argument it would be necessary to determine what factors influence the preservation of peace and then to consider whether the two situations are similar in those respects. While analogical argument sometimes has weight, most of us are probably too easily impressed by it.

The Appeal to Authority

Sometimes in discussion one supports an assertion simply by quoting the opinion of a person recognized as an authority on the subject, as when one argues that there is no defense against the atomic bomb by quoting Professor Compton to that effect.

Professor Compton is not presented as a witness testifying to a fact which any physicist would be competent to observe and report, such as the fact that Uranium 235 is radioactive. He is quoted rather as an authority whose opinion on atomic warfare is entitled to respect.

Of a witness testifying to an ordinary fact we ask only that he have had an opportunity to observe the fact and that he be a person of veracity. When any person with a reputation for verac-ity testifies that he was on the scene when the accident occurred and that the car which struck the pedestrian drove on without stopping, we attach a good deal of weight to his testimony. But of a person quoted as an authority we rightfully expect much more. We wish to be assured not only that he has an adequate knowledge of the facts, but also that he is qualified to interpret them.

If John Doe is quoted as saying that the living conditions of the average Russian citizen have improved greatly during the past ten years, we wish to know a good deal about John Doe before accepting his testimony. To begin with, has he an ade-quate knowledge of the facts? How often has he been in Russia during the past ten years? How long did he stay? What parts of the country did he visit? Was he free to go where he pleased? Does he speak Russian? Has he the training in social science necessary to observe facts of this kind? And assuming that he is thoroughly acquainted with the facts, we wish to know also how sound his judgment is in interpreting the facts. Is he free from prejudice either for or against the Russian government? Has he a financial or other personal interest that might warp his judg-ment? Has he the scientific training necessary to interpret eco-nomic and sociological data?

The questions one will wish to raise in evaluating the testimony of an authority may be summarized as follows:

1. Has the authority an adequate knowledge of the facts?
   a. Has he had an opportunity to observe the facts?
   b. Is he qualified by training and experience to observe facts in this particular field?

2. Is his judgment sound?
   a. Is he free from prejudice?
   b. Has he had scientific training in this particular field?

Probably no one would prefer to accept the testimony of an authority as conclusive when it is possible to examine the evidence itself. But often the layman must form an opinion on matters too difficult or technical for anyone but an expert to understand. Of necessity we rely constantly on the advice of the lawyer, the engineer, the physician, the scientist. But we need not take it for granted that anyone whose opinion is being quoted actually is an authority. And where possible, we wish to know whether other authorities in the field agree with the one quoted.

References

Gulley, Halbert E. *Discussion, Conference, and Group Process,* New York: Holt, Rinehart and Winston, Inc., 1960, Chap. 8.

Howell, William S. and Donald K. Smith, *Discussion,* New York: The Macmillan Company, 1956, Chaps. 4–10.

McBurney, James H. and Kenneth G. Hance, *Discussion in Human Affairs,* New York: Harper & Row, Publishers, 1950, Chaps. 6–10.

Wagner, Russell H. and Carroll C. Arnold, *Handbook of Group Discussion,* Boston: Houghton Mifflin Company, 1950, Chap. 2.

CHAPTER 8

Pitfalls in Thinking

It was an optimistic philosopher who defined man as "the rational animal." We have, it is true, a preference for sound reasoning over unsound in situations where no influence is warping our judgment. Confronted by a choice between the argument that someone must have broken into the house because the lock has been forced, and the argument that probably no one has broken in because gremlins are always forcing locks, we unhesitatingly accept the former and reject the latter. But we can hardly pride ourselves on this triumph of reason. In most situations the delicate magnetic needle of reason is easily diverted from its true direction by influences having nothing to do with logic.

The preceding chapter on the role of logic in thinking suggested how we *ought* to think if we wish to reach sound conclusions. But while an elementary knowledge of logic is useful, it does not ensure straight thinking. We are emotional as well as rational in nature, and emotional factors so often influence judgment that to reason well we must know something of psychology as well as of logic.

All of us possess, in a greater or less degree, certain traits of character that make us gullible when listening to argument: we are suggestible, emotional, selfish, timid, and indolent. These traits are always likely to betray us into irrational thinking unless we are on our guard against them. And when we are expressing our own views in discussion, they tempt us into behavior that confuses the argument and makes clear thinking difficult for other members of the group.

Why We Are Gullible

SUGGESTIBILITY. We have a tendency to believe almost anything we are told, especially if we are told it often enough by persons we like or admire. We properly attach a good deal of weight to the judgment of a recognized authority on a subject, but often we do not stop to inquire into the qualifications of the person who is speaking or is being quoted. Some people are impressed by almost anything said by an eminent person. Because George Washington warned us against "entangling alliances," some Americans oppose the North Atlantic Pact Organization. Because an industrial leader has built up a million-dollar business, he becomes for some an authority on all subjects from modern art to international relations.

A familiar variation of the "famous person" fallacy in thinking is the assumption that whatever one sees in print must be true. No touchstone of truth is more fallible than "I saw it in the paper." It is true that we depend on the printed page for most of our information, but only the critical reader separates the wheat from the chaff—and there is a bushel of chaff for each grain of wheat. Probably no view is so ill informed or absurd that it has not at some time found its way into print.

While we are too easily impressed by what eminent persons say, we are also susceptible to suggestion from persons like ourselves if they succeed in catching our attention. The ability to wear red suspenders, chew tobacco, and talk in a folksy drawl seems a slight qualification for public office, but apparently it impresses many voters. On a somewhat higher level most of us are favorably impressed by a public leader who looks and acts like one of ourselves. "Good old George," we feel, can hardly be mistaken. This may be called the "just folks" fallacy.

We are especially impressed by what ordinary people say if many of them say it. If "they say" that the world is flat, as "they" once did, no further evidence is required. On practical matters within the range of his own observation and experience the average man often thinks shrewdly and independently; his opinion on such matters, if shared by many, is entitled to respect. But on other subjects the mass of men have often been unanimously and tragically wrong. The assumption that what "they say" must be true we may label the "band wagon" fallacy.

Closely allied to the "band wagon" fallacy is the "forefather" fallacy: the assumption that whatever our forefathers believed must be true. By a strange quirk of the mind we regard earlier generations as older and wiser than our own. Actually they were younger. We have their experience and our own as well to instruct us and "because Grandfather thought so" is seldom a valid reason for thinking so now.

Especially potent is suggestion from the closely knit social and special-interest groups to which we belong—our church, lodge, club, or political party. When such groups have an official "party line," most of the members accept it without question. And even when the group takes no official stand on controversial questions, its members usually share the same opinions and prejudices. To challenge or even to question them would make us uncomfortable, and a reasonable degree of conformity is accepted by most people as the price of membership. Seldom do we join such a group because we approve of what it stands for; usually we are born into the group or join it for social reasons and then accept uncritically the opinions and attitudes of its members.

Our susceptibility to suggestion from eminent persons, from the printed page, from persons like ourselves, from the majority, from tradition, and from the groups to which we belong explains a good deal of our gullibility.

EMOTIONALISM. Any emotional state warps judgment. When a person says, "I am so angry I can't see straight," he really means, "I am so angry I can't think straight." And he is right. No one can think clearly while angry—or while jealous or afraid or carried away with enthusiasm. The emotional state blinds us to all argument not in harmony with it.

As we cannot change our nature in this respect, our only hope of thinking rationally lies in avoiding emotion when we have thinking to do. This we can accomplish to some extent by being on guard against those influences that throw us into emotional states.

Among the influences we must guard against, one, of course, is the obvious emotional appeal, as when a speaker or writer prefaces his argument on our policy toward Russia with a dramatic account of alleged brutalities committed by Russian soldiers against defenseless peasants. Even if true, the story has little bearing on the problem of foreign policy; its only purpose is to make it difficult for us to approach the problem objectively. There are times, to be sure, when we should gladly surrender to an emotional appeal. Our minds are made up, the time for action has arrived; and the speaker or writer who can fire us with enthusiasm to do what we already know ought to be done performs a useful service. But when we have a problem to solve, our habitual reaction to the emotional appeal should be to identify it for what it is and to ignore it as completely as possible.

More insidious than the frank emotional appeal, because more subtle, is the use by a speaker or writer of words, phrases, and other symbols that touch off strong emotional reactions. Such terms as *radical, liberal, conservative, socialism, communism, Americanism, free enterprise, bureaucracy*; such symbols as the flag, the national anthem, the hammer and sickle—all are capable of provoking an emotional response in most people. And all are used deliberately for that purpose by the propagandist. The critical reader or listener detects the use of such emotionally loaded words at once, and recognizing them for what they are, is largely immune to their influence.

In discussion we are likely also to respond emotionally to any remark that contradicts what we have said, that questions our motives, or that seems in any other way to attack us personally. Our resentment against the speaker then blinds us to the merit we might otherwise see in his argument. To think clearly in discussion we must cultivate the habit of studiously ignoring the emotional implications of the other person's provocative language.

If we are to be cool and objective in our thinking, then, we must be on our guard against reacting to emotional appeals, emotionally loaded words, and provocative statements.

SELFISHNESS. Our capacity for believing whatever serves our own interest is remarkable. In other people the defect is obvious. When a prosperous physician opposes public medicine, a wealthy manufacturer favors protective tariff, a laborer advocates social security, or a dairy farmer defends taxing oleomargine, we say, "Naturally—he is prejudiced." But we all have the same blind spot.

And we are all under the same illusion of objectivity. The physician opposes public medicine on the ground that it would hamper medical research; the dairy farmer favors taxing oleomargarine because the tax would discourage the growing of soybeans and thus conserve the soil. Seldom is any intentional dishonesty involved. We accept the conclusion that favors our interest and then discover or invent "reasons" to support it. This process of inventing reasons to support a conclusion already accepted without evidence is sometimes called *rationalization*. Where our interest is involved we can guard against the tendency to rationalize by asking ourselves the question: If my interest were not involved, would I consider this a sound argument?

TIMIDITY. No one defends timidity as a trait of character, but few appreciate how much it influences thinking. It warps our judgment in at least three ways.

We all fear the unknown and therefore dread change, often quite unreasonably. Any proposal involving a sharp break with familiar ways of thinking or acting is suspect, and we immediately warn the innovator against "jumping from the frying pan into the fire." The warning is in order only after we have carefully considered the probable consequences, good and bad, of the proposed change. To shun the new simply because it is new is not prudence, but timidity.

For much the same reason we fear "extreme" measures and prefer keeping to the middle of the road. That following the middle of the road is always the safest course is an illusion. It implies that of two divergent courses of action both contain good and evil, which is not always true, and that a middle course will combine the good and avoid the evil of both, which also is not always true. It is doubtful, for example, whether any middle course is possible between authoritarianism and democracy. This does not imply that extreme measures are preferable to moderation; it does imply that before choosing a middle course we should examine the evidence. Sometimes it is only timidity that keeps us in the middle of the road.

And we dread doubt and suspense. For this reason we find fence sitting painful and often fly prematurely to one conclusion or another just to get the matter settled. This may settle our minds, but it does not settle the problem. When the evidence does not justify a conclusion, no conclusion should be drawn; rather we should withhold judgment until more evidence is found.

While we cannot altogether overcome our timidity, we can think more rationally by guarding against the "conservative" fallacy, the "middle of the road" fallacy, and the fallacy of "jumping to conclusions."

INDOLENCE. Thinking is hard work. Most of us avoid it when we can; and when we must think, we take any short cut that promises a conclusion without serious effort. Unfortunately some of the short cuts involve very bad thinking.

We are too lazy, for example, to search until we find the word or phrase that exactly fits the idea we wish to express. We speak vaguely of "government in business" when we mean "government regulation of public utility rates." For "ratification of the treaty by the Senate" we are content to say, "passage of the treaty by Congress." To think in this bumbling fashion is like trying to thread a needle while wearing boxing gloves. In a given context no two words convey exactly the same meaning, and loose, vague phraseology does not amount to the same thing as more precise expression of the idea.

The use of the right word is not only essential to the successful communication of ideas to others, it is essential to the clarity of thought itself. Until we have put an idea into precise language, we do not clearly understand the idea; we have in mind only a rough approximation of it. It is impossible, therefore, to divorce precision of expression from clarity of thought. In thinking it is the beginning of wisdom to use the right word and to know what we mean by it, and this requires more effort than we are sometimes willing to make.

Indolence is responsible also for a tendency to oversimplification in thinking. It requires a painful effort to keep in mind and to take account of the complexities that make up the Chinese situation. Unwilling to make the effort, we indulge in a kind of headline thinking which ignores the bothersome details: the Nationalist regime, we say, is corrupt, the Chinese Communist party is run by Russia, the Chinese peasants are incapable of self-government. In real life no situation is that simple, and to think in headlines is to miss most of the truth.

Another form of oversimplification is the tendency to regard a complex situation or proposal as either entirely good or entirely bad. It is probable that a system of public medicine would have both desirable and undesirable features. After a careful examination of both one might conclude that the desirable features outweigh the undesirable (or vice versa), but to assume at any stage of one's thinking that such a measure is either entirely good or entirely bad prevents any real consideration of the problem. The "black or white" short cut never leads to a sound conclusion.

Still another form of oversimplification consists in personifying abstractions. In thinking of Russia it is difficult to keep in mind the many peoples, official personalities, cultural traditions, economic practices, and political forms that make up the Soviet Union. We find it easier to ignore these complexities and think of the Russian Premier as Russia. When he speaks, Russia is speaking; what he thinks, Russia thinks. Though vaguely aware that this assumption is nonsense, we constantly allow it to influence our thinking.

Vagueness and oversimplification are not the only errors into which indolence betrays us. Reference has already been made to the fact that we often reject a new idea because we fear change. Conversely, we are inclined to accept without examination any new idea that fits neatly into our familiar pattern of thinking and acting. To a person reared in the American democratic tradition and accustomed to the American form of government the suggestion that the people of Indonesia should adopt a similar political system seems plausible enough. "Why not?" we ask, and accept the idea forthwith. To inquire into the political needs, capacities, and resources of the Indonesian people and to consider what form of government would best serve their interests would require an effort we are unwilling to make.

Finally, because of indolence we often abandon entirely the attempt to solve a problem that proves difficult. After examining some of the evidence and finding it contradictory or inconclusive, we shrug our shoulders and say, "Well, you can't tell what to think, can you?" And we dismiss the problem from our minds. This fault is as serious as the opposite one, noted above, of jumping prematurely to a conclusion. When we drop an unsolved problem, we can seldom claim to be withholding judgment while we seek further evidence; usually we make no attempt to find more evidence and simply lapse into indifference. We often need the courage to withhold judgment, but we need also the *will to find out.*

It is discouraging to realize how often our suggestibility, emotionalism, selfishness, timidity, and indolence warp our thinking. And it is disturbing to know that the propagandist deliberately plays upon these weaknesses to serve his own ends. But to be forewarned is to be forearmed. We can avoid many of these pitfalls by being on guard against them.

Developing Immunity to Propaganda

Any discussion of propaganda is embarrassed by the fact that the word *propaganda* has fallen on evil days. Originally the word meant simply any activity or discourse, oral or written, intended to influence others toward a particular view, especially when the writer or speaker is frankly partisan and makes no attempt to present both sides of the case. There can be no objection to propaganda in this sense; partisan persuasive speaking and writing is an essential part of the democratic process. But to many the word now implies that the speaker or writer conceals the fact that his motive is partisan and attempts to hide under a cloak of objectivity; to some it implies also that he deliberately makes dishonest or misleading statements. We should of course be on our guard against propaganda in this sense, and unfortunately much of what we hear and read is propaganda in the sense that the speaker or writer attempts to conceal the fact that he is inspired by partisan motives.

One of the best safeguards against being misled by propaganda is of course to examine arguments and appeals objectively and on their merit, so that we do not fall into the pitfalls discussed earlier in this chapter. But it helps also to consider the source of the appeal. Who made the statement and who is he? Is he a scholar of such reputation that his objectivity can be assumed? Is he presenting one side only of the issue discussed? Do his background and organizational connections suggest that he is more partisan in motive than he admits? Can his statements of fact be verified? Often our questions about the source of an appeal cannot be answered satisfactorily because the appeal is anonymous. Such appeals should always be regarded as highly suspect.

How We Obstruct Group Thinking

We have noted that certain traits in human character make us an easy prey to specious argument and that the propagandist sometimes plays upon these weaknesses to influence our thinking. It would be a mistake to suppose, however, that appeals which warp our thinking are always made with deliberate intent to mislead. Some of the very traits that make us gullible also betray us into discussion behavior that makes it difficult for others in the group to think straight. And against this tendency also we should be on our guard. At the risk of repeating some of the suggestions already made in Chapter 5, we may note some of the ways in which we unintentionally obstruct the thinking of others.

There are four easy ways to be a nuisance in discussion: failing to listen to or to understand what others are saying, being careless in the use of language, lacking candor in appraising argument, and lacking objectivity.

FAILURE TO LISTEN. In discussion we are sometimes too impatient to speak or too preoccupied with our own thoughts to listen carefully to what is being said. Only half understanding the point that has been made, we attempt to reply immediately —and our irrelevant remark throws the discussion off the track. But our failure to understand is not always due to inattention; sometimes it is due to a hostility toward the speaker that leads us unintentionally to distort what he has said. The following passage is typical of what often happens in discussion.

Jones: I don't think it is fair to require a public schoolteacher to swear that he is not a Communist. We don't require—

Smith: So it's unfair to keep Communists out of the schools! You would let them convert our children to communism! Well, there we disagree.

Jones: That isn't what I said. . . .

Jones is quite right—that is *not* what he said. Smith's hostility has betrayed him, perhaps unconsciously, into distorting Jones's statement and setting up in place of what Jones really meant a straw man that can be attacked more easily. The result may be to throw the entire group into confusion for five or ten minutes.

CARELESS USE OF LANGUAGE. We have already noted that the use of vague, poorly defined words and phrases confuses our own thinking. It also confuses the thinking of those who listen to us. If a speaker says "play Santa Claus to the world" when he means "appropriate funds for technical assistance," no one will understand what he means, and the ensuing discussion will probably lapse into confusion.

Careless use of language is illustrated also by the tendency to reckless overstatement. A speaker means to say, "Some forms of national advertising are probably not conducive to the public welfare." Excited or annoyed, he actually says, "Advertising is a public menace." Exaggeration provoking exaggeration, the next speaker retorts, "On the contrary, modern industrial civilization is based on advertising."

The business of a discussion group can be transacted only in the currency of a common language understood by all, and those who carelessly or recklessly debase the currency are enemies of group thinking. If they are to think together, the members of a discussion group must know what they mean and say what they mean.

LACK OF CANDOR. Ideally all members of a discussion group understand that the discussion is off the record, that no one loses face when he changes his mind, that in fact willingness to change one's mind is a virtue. This perfect candor is seldom achieved. When the position a member has taken proves untenable or an argument he has advanced is shown to be weak, instead of admitting his error and modifying his thinking, he is likely to feel that honor does not permit him to acknowledge the error. Unable to meet the argument against him, he tries to evade it by changing the subject, by obscuring the issue in a cloud of words, or by surreptitiously shifting his ground. This delays and confuses the thinking of the entire group.

LACK OF OBJECTIVITY. Much has already been said about the ways in which lack of objectivity vitiates our own thinking. It also leads us into discussion behavior that obstructs the thinking of others. In the excitement of discussion, for example, we may use loaded words that set off emotional reactions in others and thus bias their thinking. If we are opposed to public medicine, we refer to it, with prejudicial emphasis, as "socialized" medicine. The appointment to the Supreme Court of a jurist of whose political philosophy we disapprove we refer to as "packing" the Court. One contribution each member of a group can make to clear thinking by his colleagues is to avoid the use of emotionally loaded words and phrases.

Another contribution each member can make to clear thinking by others is to control his own temper. An ill-tempered outburst by one member provokes a similar reaction in others, and soon no one can think rationally. If another member loses his temper or is in some other way offensive, it is a good rule not to reply immediately but to consider why he feels so strongly. This cools one's own temper. And when tempted to explode, it is also wholesome to remember that losing one's temper is usually a confession that one has no real argument to present. We don't usually explode except when we feel strongly and are aware that we can make no convincing defense of our position.

Finally, we should avoid obstructing the thinking of our colleagues by criticizing their motives rather than their arguments. Confronted with the argument that the St. Lawrence–Great Lakes Waterway was exorbitantly expensive, we say, "So you are from New York City? I understand why you New Yorkers don't like the Waterway—it takes business away from New York Harbor." This remark has no bearing whatever on the cost of the waterway, and its only effect is to annoy the other person and divert attention from the point under discussion.

We should be on our guard, then, not only against influences that bias our own thinking, but also against the tendency to express ourselves in such a way as to bias the thinking of others. Our tendency to stumble into the pitfalls discussed in this chapter arises from our psychological make-up rather than from our ignorance of logic. We cannot change our nature, but by knowing what warps thinking we can often avoid it.

References

Burtt, Edwin A., *Right Thinking*, New York: Harper & Row, Publishers, 1946.

Childs, Harwood L., *An Introduction to Public Opinion*, New York: John Wiley & Sons, Inc., 1940.

Doob, Leonard W., *Public Opinion and Propaganda,* New York: Holt, Rinehart and Winston, Inc., 1948.

Hayakawa, S. I., *Language in Action,* New York: Harcourt, Brace & World, Inc., 1941.

Lasker, Bruno, *Democracy Through Discussion,* New York: H. W. Wilson Co., 1949, Chap. 8.

Thouless, Robert H., *How To Think Straight,* New York: Simon and Schuster, Inc., 1939.

PART THREE

PUTTING
DISCUSSION TO WORK

CHAPTER 9

The Community Round Table

No community should be without one or more groups meeting regularly for the informal discussion of public questions. Whether they confine their attention to local problems or discuss national and international questions as well, such groups are an essential part of the democratic process at the community level. Every citizen should belong to one; if he can find none in his neighborhood, he should try to organize one.

Organizing a Discussion Group

Is there an organization in the community that would be interested in devoting meetings regularly or occasionally to the discussion of public questions? If so, it is usually better to work through such an organization than to start a new one. Members of the existing organization are accustomed to meeting regularly; they have a feeling of loyalty to the group; they are already acquainted with one another. These are important factors in the success of a discussion program. It takes time and labor to build up a new organization, and the mortality rate of such groups is high.

But if no organization in the community is interested in discussion, one should not hesitate to start a new one. Usually it is best to start in a small way and very informally. A good method is to invite a half dozen interested friends to one's home for an evening to discuss some public question in which they are interested. If the meeting is successful, another should be held a month later with a few additional guests. Most discussion groups have grown out of such informal semisocial gatherings. The number of members need not be large; six or eight are enough, and for good discussion the group should never exceed twenty. Formal organization and a public meeting place are seldom necessary.

In organizing a group the following suggestions may prove useful. Prepare carefully for the first meeting. Make clear to those attending that they are not coming to hear a speech but to do their own talking. Select for discussion a problem in which the members are interested, one on which they have opinions, and one on which there will be some difference of opinion among them. And choose as leader someone whom the group likes and respects and who will be willing to prepare for the meeting. If the venture succeeds, provision should be made soon to train those who are to serve as leaders.

Preparing for Discussion

PRELIMINARIES. The topic for discussion should be selected well in advance of the meeting, consideration being given to the suggestions in Chapter 2 on the conditions necessary for good discussion. Early arrangements should also be made for a meeting place where all who are likely to attend can be seated comfortably.

Announcement of the question to be discussed may be made at a previous meeting of the group, but usually telephone calls or a postal card or form letter will result in better attendance. If possible, the announcement should state the question to be discussed and the agenda to be followed, should indicate the time and place of the meeting, and should mention the name of the discussion leader. The tone of the announcement should be informal, as in this example:

How should we handle the housing problem?
1. Can private industry solve the problem?
2. Would voluntary cooperative housing projects help?
3. Should the government assist by
     a. Extending credit to private builders?
     b. Building government housing units?
Let's talk it over next Wednesday, February 11, 8 P.M. at the home of William Beck, 19 Wetmore Road. Mr. Carl Smith will lead the discussion.

If a more extended announcement is to be made through a form letter, it might include such additional material as a provocative statement of fact, a challenging quotation, perhaps a short list of some of the arguments on either side of the question. It might also list several magazine articles on the subject. Anything that arouses interest in advance helps to ensure a lively discussion.

INFORMATION. Chapter 2 suggests several methods of making available to a group the information it must have to discuss any question intelligently. While one should not overlook any method of providing information, the leader of a community round table will often find that he must himself be the group's principal source of information. If so, he must study the question in preparation for leading the discussion. In this connection he may find the suggestions in Chapter 3 useful.

AGENDA. When the leader has obtained a sufficient knowledge of the question, he should prepare an agenda. In Chapter 4 it was suggested that the group itself should work out the agenda, and in many situations this is sound practice. But it takes a good deal of time; a group devoting several sessions to discussion of a problem will probably need most of the first session to arrive at a satisfactory agenda. A citizens' round table can usually devote one session only to discussion of each problem; if it must work out its own agenda, little time will be left for discussion of the issues. It is wise, therefore, for the discussion leader to prepare an agenda. If possible, it should be written on a blackboard, where members of the group can glance at it during the discussion.

An agenda should not be imposed on the group against its will, however. Unless members are satisfied that it represents a sound analysis of the problem, they will have little confidence in the conclusions reached. In presenting an agenda, the leader should inquire whether any member has in mind an argument relevant to discussion of the question which cannot be brought up under one or another of the issues proposed. If so, the agenda should be revised until all are satisfied with it. Usually if the leader has worked out an agenda carefully, the group will be glad to accept it.

INTRODUCTORY TALK. If the group is meeting to continue discussion of a problem to which several sessions are being devoted, the leader should open the session with a brief statement of the result of discussion at previous sessions and indicate what issues are to be considered at the present meeting. Most community round tables devote one session only to consideration of a question, and the leader's task in opening the meeting is to introduce the question and present such material as will pave the way for profitable discussion. This is best done by means of a ten- or fifteen-minute talk.

The talk may begin with a few remarks designed to arouse interest in the problem and sharpen realization of its importance. An arresting quotation or a reference to a recent event will sometimes serve. The question to be discussed is then stated. This may involve defining terms; for example, if the question is whether Congress should adopt a system of public medicine, it would be well to define "public medicine." Much confusion and waste of time will be avoided if all understand from the beginning precisely what is to be discussed.

If the question is one of those characterized in Chapter 2 as a problem of personal conduct, it can often be put before the group most effectively in dramatic form. The leader prepares in brief story form a real or fictitious case presenting the problem to be discussed. Such a dramatic presentation of the problem should usually be made immediately after the leader has stated the question.

In introducing the discussion of most public problems, the leader will not find the case method useful and will proceed from statement of the question to a statement of whatever background of fact may be necessary for intelligent discussion. It may be useful to state briefly the facts out of which the problem has arisen or to review previous attempts to solve it. No one set of topics can be followed invariably. The leader should present whatever material will best set the stage for profitable discussion. Most groups value a good expository statement; it provides a sound foundation for discussion and gives them something to carry away with them. And even the well-informed are usually glad to have the principal facts reviewed briefly.

An exposition of facts should seldom consume more than ten minutes. If twenty or thirty minutes are required, the topic probably is not suitable for discussion by this particular group. Few persons can assimilate a large body of new information at one sitting well enough to make any practical use of it in discussion.

And the factual statement should be strictly impartial. To slant it toward any particular solution of the problem destroys its value as a basis for discussion and weakens confidence in the leader's integrity.

After the leader has presented his expository statement, he should close his introductory talk by presenting the agenda for approval by the group.

The topics, then, which the leader will often wish to cover in introducing a public question for discussion are these:

1. Opening remarks to arouse interest in the problem
2. Statement of the question
3. Statement of the facts
4. Presentation of the agenda

While the leader will deliver the introductory talk with little or no interruption by the group, he should not think of it as a formal speech. He should remain seated while talking and speak as informally as he will do while moderating the discussion to follow. In no circumstances should the talk be written out and read. The leader should outline it carefully on one or two sheets of paper and speak from notes. The inexperienced speaker will find that talking the material through aloud several times will help to fix the sequence of ideas in mind and develop fluency in their expression. In any case he should be so familiar with the outline that he need do no more than glance at it occasionally as he presents the talk.

Conducting the Session

Little need be added here to what has already been said in Chapter 6 on moderating discussion. The leader will invite discussion in turn on each of the issues in the agenda, pointing up the discussion as it proceeds and summing it up at the end of the session. He may find that discussion is livelier if in proposing each issue for consideration he suggests some of the arguments on either side. This "primes the pump" and discussion gets under way more rapidly.

At the close of the session the leader should usually invite the group to consider what action it wishes to take as a result of the discussion. In some cases it may take collective action; in others individual members may wish to act by expressing their views at the polls, by writing to their congressman, or by circulating a petition. Whether agreement has been reached or not, the members should be encouraged to give appropriate expression in action to whatever views they hold. And the leader should be prepared to assist them. He should be prepared, for example, to tell them who their congressmen are and how to address letters to them. The interest and conviction generated by a good discussion should not be allowed to evaporate without finding effective expression.

In conducting a community round table two problems not considered in Chapter 6 may arise. One concerns the use of time. While discussion usually should not run for more than an hour and a half, no public question can be discussed adequately in that length of time. If the entire agenda is to be covered, the leader must terminate discussion of some of the issues before agreement has been reached. Would it be preferable to give to each issue the time necessary to reach agreement, even if some issues are not touched? The leader may wish to put this question to the group before discussion starts. If it is left to his own judgment, he will usually find that the group is better satisfied when it covers the entire agenda, even though some issues are discussed inadequately.

Another problem arises when the group is affiliated with a national organization which takes an official stand on the question discussed. The League of Women Voters of the United States, for example, has committed itself on some questions which its local leagues may still wish to discuss. How can the leader of such a group be strictly impartial in presenting the introductory talk and moderating discussion and still do justice to the stand taken by the national organization?

A partial solution perhaps would be to confine discussion to questions on which the national organization has not taken a stand. The organization may be committed to support of the United Nations, but within the limits of that commitment innumerable controversial questions arise which are suitable for discussion. Some national organizations wisely invite their local groups to study and discuss a problem before an official position is taken.

But suppose that the group does discuss a question on which its national organization has announced an official stand. The leader wishes to do justice to his work as moderator and yet to state and defend the position of the organization. Probably the best solution is for him to remain strictly impartial until the group has concluded its discussion and then to state and defend the view of the organization, perhaps relating it to the conclusions, sound or unsound (in the leader's view), at which the group has arrived.

But even when this is done, may not members carry away with them the wrong conclusion? They certainly may. This is one of the hazards of democracy for those convinced that they already know the right answers; when we invite people to think, we run the risk of their reaching conclusions we do not like. But this should not disturb us. If a cause is sound it cannot help profiting in the long run from the freest possible discussion. To believe otherwise is to lack faith in democracy.

Presenting the Problem Dramatically

THE USE OF FILMS. Earlier in the chapter it was suggested that a problem can sometimes be presented effectively in story form. From the story to the motion picture is a natural step; and when the right film can be found, there is no more effective way to present a problem for discussion. The films employed for the purpose are usually 16-mm black-and-white sound films running from ten to twenty minutes. Many of them can be rented at public libraries, and often a projector and screen can be borrowed from the local high school or from a church in the community. The film department of any large public library is a good source of information about such films.

When a film is to be used, the leader should arrange in advance to have someone other than himself operate the projector. The operator should be thoroughly familiar with the machine and should have the projector and screen set up in advance. Delay in getting the meeting under way is one of the surest ways to kill group interest.

The following outline may be useful in conducting the session:

1. Make a few introductory remarks, stating the question to be discussed in as interesting a manner as possible.
2. Show the film.
3. Make a short talk (three or four minutes), summarizing the film contents and presenting the agenda to be followed.
4. Lead the group in discussion of each of the issues in the agenda.
5. Sum up the discussion.

ROLE PLAYING. Often when the problem concerns human relations, it can be presented effectively in an eight- to ten-minute skit in which several group members play the roles involved. Suppose, for example, that a group of teachers and parents are to discuss a disciplinary problem that often arises in a local high school. One member plays the role of an adolescent girl whose behavior presents the problem, another the role of a teacher, and a third the role of the student's mother. The scene takes place in the teacher's classroom after school hours with the three characters present for a conference. The lines spoken by the characters are not determined in advance; rather each role player says and does what she feels she would really say and do in the actual situation, not even the role players knowing in advance just how the skit will come out. When the skit has run long enough to present the problem, the leader interrupts it and the group proceeds to discussion of the problem, talking largely in terms of the skit presented and of what the role players said and did.

The leader and the role players should have had a brief session in advance, in which it is made clear to each player who he is supposed to be, and each is given a conception of the background of the person he is to portray. Each is then instructed to project himself into the role and to improvise what he says and does as he goes along.

The dramatic presentation of a problem, when this is feasible, usually results in a more lively and interesting discussion than when the problem is presented abstractly.

Adapting Discussion to a Large Group

The methods recommended in this book will not be found satisfactory for groups of more than twenty or twenty-five persons. In a larger group real conversation is hardly possible, and the most that can be expected is forum discussion, in which some members of the audience participate by addressing questions to a speaker or by expressing their own views in short speeches. Such discussion may of course be profitable, especially if preceded by a systematic presentation of the subject by one or more well-informed speakers; but there is increasing demand for a procedure suitable for large groups that will preserve at least some of the values of round-table discussion. Two such procedures are available.

MULTIPLE ROUND TABLES. If all members of a large group wish to participate actively in discussion, they should be divided for a part of the session into several small groups. The person in charge of the meeting delivers to the entire group the introductory talk referred to earlier in the chapter and closes his statement by proposing an agenda. The group then breaks up into smaller units of eight or ten each, which meet separately for an hour of informal discussion. During this period each unit follows the agenda under the guidance of its own moderator. The group then reassembles. Each leader reports briefly on the result of discussion in his unit, after which all participate for twenty minutes in general discussion addressed primarily to those points on which the subgroups have reached contradictory conclusions. The person in charge of the meeting presides over the forum and at its close sums up the consensus of the entire group as it has been revealed in the leaders' reports and in the general discussion.

The success of this method obviously depends very much on the competence of the leaders assigned to moderate discussion in the small groups. If they are selected at random without reference to their qualifications, the results will be disappointing. An organization wishing to employ the method regularly should make provision for recruiting and training a staff of moderators. When such provision is made, the method can be highly satisfactory. It has been used successfully with groups of a hundred, and presumably the number could be even larger.

In some cases the seating arrangement may present a problem. When the larger group breaks up after the introductory talk, smaller groups may adjourn to nearby rooms for the informal discussion period and then reassemble for the closing forum discussion. This is reasonably satisfactory if enough small rooms are available, but adjourning and reassembling consume time and cause some noise and confusion. If the assembly room is large enough, it is perhaps better to provide in that room enough tables, each seating eight or ten, to accommodate the entire membership. The tables should of course be placed far enough apart to ensure that groups do not interfere with each other. Members seat themselves at the tables as they enter the room and remain in their places during the entire session. All three parts of the program are then provided for without the necessity of shifting chairs or leaving the room.

PANEL DISCUSSION. In another adaptation of discussion procedure to a large group, a panel of from four to eight persons and a moderator are seated on the platform in a semicircle facing the audience. After the moderator has presented the introductory statement, he leads the panel in discussion while the audience listens. Usually he reserves a half hour at the close of the panel discussion for questions and remarks from the audience, or he interrupts the panel at convenient points to permit a few minutes of audience participation. During both panel discussion and audience participation the tone of the meeting should be informal, and panel members should remain seated while speaking.

This method also has been used widely and with marked success. Its value depends very much on the competence of the panel. It should represent a diversity of background and viewpoint, and its members must speak up with enough animation to be heard by the audience and hold its interest. It is well for the moderator to meet with panel members in advance to acquaint them with the procedure to be followed and with the agenda. In some cases he may wish to have their advice in drawing up the agenda. Usually members of a panel are experts on the problem to be discussed, though well-informed laymen are sometimes also useful.

Perhaps the difficulties most often encountered are that panel members deliver speeches to the audience instead of discussing the question among themselves, or that they forget the audience entirely and fail to make themselves heard. These difficulties can usually be avoided if the moderator discusses procedure with the panel in advance.

THE BUZZ SESSION. Occasionally the chairman in charge of a program before an audience feels that all of those present would have something to contribute or he wishes for some reason to involve all in the discussion to at least some extent. The group is too large for informal discussion in the ordinary sense, but the method of multiple round tables does not seem feasible. And the purpose of the meeting is merely to collect ideas for later evaluation rather than to attempt methodical discussion of a problem. For example, a group of a hundred or more experienced librarians are devoting a session to the question: How can the librarian make the resources of the library more widely available to members of the community? All may be expected to have something to contribute, and the only purpose is to collect ideas for later sifting and evaluation by a committee.

In this situation the chairman may divide the audience quickly into small groups of six each by asking all of those in the first, third, fifth row and other alternate rows to turn in their seats facing those directly behind them. He then suggests that the three on the first row at his extreme right and the three they are now facing consider themselves a discussion group of six with the one to the chairman's right who has turned around serving as leader and the one next to him as secretary. And so on throughout the auditorium. The entire audience is now divided into groups of six without the necessity of anyone's leaving his seat. Each group is then asked to think up and jot down as many ideas as possible for making the resources of a library more widely available and then to pick out what they regard as their three best suggestions. After about ten minutes the chairman calls the meeting to order and all turn around facing the front. Each group secretary then reads his group's three best suggestions while a stenographer on the platform writes them down. The procedure is likely to result in a hundred or more suggestions which a committee later can sift and set in order for a statement to be mimeographed and mailed out to all members.

The buzz session also is often useful when a lecture is to be followed by a question period. The chairman may fear that most members of the audience will be too shy to ask questions and that the question period will be a failure. He therefore announces that following the address the audience will be divided into buzz groups for ten minutes, each group to select the two or three questions they would most like to hear the speaker answer. Those too shy to speak up before the entire audience will seldom hesitate to express themselves in a group of six. The buzz session will probably result in many good questions, which the spokesmen of the groups in turn will address to the speaker.

References

Dale, Edgar, *Audio-Visual Methods in Teaching*, New York: Holt, Rinehart and Winston, Inc., 1946.

Gulley, Halbert E., *Discussion, Conference, and Group Process*, New York: Holt, Rinehart and Winston, Inc., 1960, Chap. 16.

Klein, Alan F., *Role Playing*, New York: Association Press, 1956.

Making Films Work for Your Community, prepared by The Committee on Community Use of Films, New York: Educational Film Library Association, 1946.

Schacht, Robert H., *How to Conduct a Community Film Forum*, Film Council of America, 6 West Ontario Street, Chicago 10, Illinois.

Strauss, L. H. and J. R. Kidd, *Look, Listen and Learn*, New York: Association Press, 1948, Chap. 9.

CHAPTER 10

Radio and Television Discussion

The informal face-to-face discussion in small groups with which we are concerned in this book has little in common with public discussion as carried on through such mediums of mass communication as radio and television. Yet one form—the panel discussion suggested at the close of the preceding chapter—is readily adapted to broadcasting and is increasingly popular. The "Chicago Round Table of the Air" and the "Northwestern Reviewing Stand" are heard nationally, and many local stations regularly present similar programs. Widely accepted as sound public education, they are, when well conducted, more interesting than most other forms of discussion on the air.

A panel discussion is a program of informal conversation, usually thirty minutes in length, on a topic of public interest. Usually the panel consists of three or four members and a leader, who prepared the program and moderates the discussion. This arrangement seems to be identical with that already considered in Chapter 9—conversation by a small group for the benefit of a larger group which listens. But while the situations have much in common and most of the suggestions of the preceding chapter are applicable to discussion on the air, there are also important differences between the two forms.

It must be understood, for example, that the purpose of radio discussion is not to reach agreement among panel members. In the brief period of time available for discussion it is not to be expected that any member will change his opinion. Nor is it desirable that he should; in most cases he is on the panel to represent a particular point of view, and the argument will be presented and criticized more effectively if no agreement is reached. The purpose of the discussion is not to resolve differences of opinion in the panel, but to interest and inform the listener or viewer and to clarify his thinking. Ignoring this and other conditions peculiar to the situation may result in a program unintelligible or uninteresting to the audience. We shall consider in turn radio and television programs.

The special problems that arise in radio discussion concern preparation of the program, the procedure followed in a broadcasting studio, and the conduct of discussion by participants and moderator.[1]

Preparation of a Radio Program

THE TOPIC. Radio discussion may be either informational or controversial. When a psychiatrist, a public health officer, and a judge discuss mental ill health as a public problem, there may be little difference of opinion among them regarding the seriousness of the problem or the measures required to solve it. The purpose of the discussion is to sharpen awareness of the problem on the part of the public, to present useful information regarding it, and to suggest some of the considerations involved in its solution. Low-cost government housing invites more sharply controversial discussion. By appointing to the panel a real estate broker, a private builder, a social worker, and a government housing official it probably would be possible to ensure a sharp difference of opinion. Either type of program

[1] For many of the suggestions made in this chapter the author is indebted to Professor Harrison B. Summers, Director of the Radio Programming Division of the Department of Speech at The Ohio State University, formerly Manager of the Public Service Division of the American Broadcasting Company.

may be interesting and informative, but before the panel is selected it should be clear which type is desired.

For either type of program the topic, to hold attention, must possess some initial interest for an audience; the discussion form itself will not create interest where none exists. In this connection it should be remembered that as controversy is the most important single factor of interest, topics chosen for informational programs must be especially interesting to hold attention. Even when topics are carefully chosen, a steady diet of informational discussion will hardly build up a listening audience. Incidentally, the topic for either type of discussion challenges attention more sharply if expressed as a question: Why is mental health our number-one public health problem? Should the federal government provide low-cost housing?

SELECTING A PANEL. Advice on the selection of radio panels always seems a counsel of perfection. The perfect panel member is difficult to find, and a panel made up entirely of such members has probably not yet been heard on the air. But it is useful to know what to look for.

A panel should be composed of at least three and preferably not more than four persons in addition to the moderator. A radio audience can identify speakers only by the sound of their voices and by hearing them address each other by name. It is difficult at best for a hearer to know which member is speaking; when more than five voices are heard, it is almost impossible to identify them. For informational discussion three is a satisfactory number; four (two on each side) is perhaps preferable when the discussion is to be controversial.

If possible, avoid a panel composed entirely of inexperienced members. Ability to participate effectively in discussion grows with practice, and familiarity with the special requirements of microphone technique is desirable. The nervousness or ineptitude of one or two inexperienced members will give the moderator trouble enough; he will not wish to cope with four beginners at the same time if he can avoid it.

Regarding the panel members' intellectual equipment for

discussion, several points are worth noting. Members should be well informed on the topic. Usually they are experts on it, though a layman with a special background of experience may sometimes have much to contribute. And they should be persons with definite views on the subject. When controversial discussion is desired, care should be taken to ensure a difference of opinion within the panel; and for informational programs diversity of background and viewpoint lends richness and variety to discussion. In general, the more diversity of background and variety of resource represented in the panel, the better the discussion will be. It is desirable, however, that all of the members be operating at about the same level of intellectual sophistication; the professional economist and the "man in the street" can seldom contribute effectively to the same discussion.

The panel member's personality is also a factor in successful radio discussion. The person who is lively, articulate, and forceful, who is warm, sympathetic, and colorful, who has a gift for concrete illustration and pungent expression is a valuable member. His articulation must be reasonably good if he is to make himself understood over the air. And a good voice helps, though in this respect variety also is useful; it helps to identify the speakers. A somewhat harsh or strident voice that would be unpleasant to listen to for an hour may afford a welcome contrast to other voices on a program. The contrast between men's and women's voices serves the same purpose.

THE PRELIMINARY MEETING. It is usually a mistake to rehearse a panel discussion. Detailed knowledge in advance of what another will say and of what we will say in reply destroys spontaneity. But for certain other purposes a preliminary meeting of moderator and panel is indispensable. For one thing members need to become well enough acquainted to feel comfortable together. This suggests the desirability of meeting at the luncheon or dinner table, where conviviality can be combined with the more serious business of planning the program.

The principal purpose of the meeting is to work out a simple agenda indicating points to be covered in the discussion. The suggestions in Chapter 4 on pattern in discussion have little application here, for in a thirty-minute discussion there can be no pretense of examining the subject thoroughly. The agenda should be based rather on the following considerations: What issues will the audience wish to hear discussed? What issues is this panel most interested in discussing? On what issues does the panel have the sharpest difference of opinion?

To discover answers to the last two questions the moderator cannot do better than invite members of the panel to plunge into an exploratory discussion of the topic. If he stirs them up occasionally with a provocative question and avoids guiding conversation, he will soon learn what they wish to talk about and where they disagree. He should then interrupt their discussion and ask them to work out an agenda, giving due consideration to the information, interest, and expectation of the radio audience. The four or five points making up the agenda agreed upon should be arranged in a convenient order and phrased as questions. The moderator and panel members will have copies of this agenda before them during the broadcast. A momentary awkwardness in starting discussion of the several issues may be avoided by deciding in advance which panel member is to speak first on each issue.

If some members are inexperienced in radio discussion, the moderator should indicate the procedure to be followed in the studio and explain any hand signals he may intend to use. An elaborate system of signals is worse than useless; the inexperienced member will not remember what they mean and probably will be distracted and disconcerted by them. The following signals, however, are nearly self-explanatory, and their use helps the moderator to control the discussion without interrupting it.

While one member is speaking, another who wishes to follow holds up his forefinger, and the moderator gives him the floor in advance by pointing to him. If several raise their forefingers at the same time, the moderator indicates by pointing which is to speak next. If, while one member is speaking, the moderator glances at another with elevated eyebrow, he means to inquire,

Do you wish to come in next? The member responds by shaking his head affirmatively or negatively. If the moderator wishes to interrupt a speaker, he holds up the palm of his hand toward him, meaning: Close your present sentence quickly.

By the use of these signals the moderator will escape two difficulties not otherwise easily avoided: dead spaces in the discussion when for several moments no one speaks, and collision between two members who start to speak at the same moment. Both detract from the interest of the program.

Studio Procedure

In the broadcasting studio, members of the panel and the moderator are seated around a table with one or more microphones before them. The program announcer is stationed at another microphone in the same room. The engineer, usually visible in the control room through a soundproof window, may wish to check the voices of the speakers after they have taken their places. Each speaks a few sentences, and the position of the microphone on the table is adjusted to ensure a satisfactory balance of voices. For best results, speakers should sit well forward in their chairs with elbows on the table and when addressing each other should avoid turning their faces away from the microphone. When these precautions are observed, it is unnecessary to speak more loudly than in ordinary conversation. Care should be taken not to touch the microphone, pound the table, or rustle papers.

As the program goes on the air, a red light flashes on in the studio and the engineer points to the program announcer. The announcer introduces the program, usually mentioning the topic to be discussed and introducing the moderator. At the conclusion of his remarks he points to the moderator, who is in charge from that point on.

The moderator states the question, unless the announcer has already done so, and introduces the panel, mentioning each member by name, indicating his official position, if any, and adding a few words regarding his qualifications to discuss the

topic. In some cases he may prefer to have each member introduce himself by giving his name. The moderator then makes a
few remarks to prepare the audience for the discussion. He may,
for example, say something to arouse interest in the topic,
mention the principal issues to be covered in discussion, and
set forth some facts surrounding the problem. These introductory remarks, however, should be very brief—seldom more
than a half-dozen sentences. If many facts must be presented, it
will be more interesting to have the panel bring them out before
proceeding to the controversial issues.

It is the moderator's responsibility to distribute the available
time among various issues on the agenda, to make a one- or
two-minute summary of the discussion at the end and thank
panel members for their participation, and to return the microphone to the announcer in time for his concluding remarks. To
keep on schedule and close in time he will find it useful to have
a stop watch on the table before him. The panel must preserve
complete silence during the announcer's final remarks; the
program is on the air until the red light in the studio goes off.

Participating in the Discussion

Most of the suggestions in Chapter 5 on participating in
discussion apply to radio discussion. The participant's attitude
should be one of courtesy, geniality, and evident interest in the
topic; he should speak up freely, refrain from interrupting
others, be brief, follow the ball, and express himself without
giving unnecessary offense to those who disagree with him. But
for radio discussion some of these suggestions require special
emphasis, and several additional suggestions can be made.

On the air it is especially important that the panel member
speak up promptly, coming in immediately on the heels of the
preceding speaker; otherwise, a frequent occurrence of blank
spots in discussion makes the program drag. It is important also
that conversation be brisk. The member who hems and haws
or speaks with undue deliberation is tiresome to hear. As
naturalness and spontaneity are important virtues in a radio

program, members should speak extemporaneously and without notes and should avoid reading long quotations from their favorite authorities. Finally, they should use concrete and colorful language, working in humor and human-interest material wherever possible. Deprived of the use of gesture and facial expression as rhetorical devices, the radio speaker must be especially interesting to hold attention.

It has already been suggested that to enjoy a program fully a listener must be able to identify the speakers. Members of a panel can assist him by addressing each other by name and by frequently including in their remarks a brief reference to their own interests and background, which helps to identify the speaker, or a reference to the background or interests of the person addressed, which helps to identify the next speaker.

Moderating Discussion

In moderating radio discussion the leader will find useful the attitudes of geniality, interest, impartiality, and responsibility recommended in an earlier chapter; and he will find that his work consists essentially of regulating, focusing, guiding, clarifying, and pointing up discussion. But on the air some of these functions require special attention. For example, he must clarify discussion not only for members of the panel, but also for the unseen audience, which is less familiar with the topic than the speakers and more likely to become confused. If a member loses his temper, the moderator must step in immediately. He cannot ignore, as he may do occasionally in leading ordinary discussion, the member whose remarks are in bad taste or who speaks too long. And while he would prefer not to break in on a speaker, he must not hesitate to do so if the situation requires prompt action.

Regulating participation presents two problems peculiar to discussion on the air. When two members talk at the same time, the listening audience cannot understand what either of them is saying. Interruptions, therefore, are more serious than in ordinary discussion. The use of a simple system of hand signals helps a great deal, and the moderator may need to be more firm than in conducting discussion off the air. Blank spots, particularly, must be avoided; as the listener cannot see panel members, he loses interest immediately when no one is speaking. When a member who is to have the floor next does not speak up promptly, the moderator must step in at once to fill the gap.

Often the moderator will not know until he is on the air whether his panel members are the kind who will interrupt each other or who will be too slow in coming in. Consequently even more alertness and resource are required than in leading ordinary discussion.

Special Problems and Procedures in Television Discussion

Much of the advice given above for radio discussion holds equally of discussion before television cameras. But the camera introduces a number of special difficulties which both moderator and panelists may at first find disconcerting. To some of these problems no completely satisfactory solution has yet been found.

One becomes accustomed to the extremely bright overhead lights in a television studio, but the gyrations of usually two or more camera men wheeling their cameras about in front of the group is more distracting. They wish some of the time to be far enough away to take in the group as a whole but also wish, so far as possible, to have a close-up view of each member as he speaks. This involves rapid and almost continuous moving of cameras. Group members should ignore the cameras and especially should avoid looking into a camera. They will make life easier for the camera men, however, if they address each other by name when they put a question to or reply to another member; this makes it easier for the camera men to foresee who is likely to speak next.

Somewhere in front of the group but out of camera range a station staff member is likely now and then to make hand signals to the moderator warning him how much time remains for the program; the moderator must therefore frequently glance out of the corner of his eye away from the group, preferably when the camera is not trained on him, to make sure he sees these signals.

Perhaps most disconcerting is the fact that everything the group does is seen as well as heard. The moderator therefore cannot employ hand signals, as he often does in radio discussion, and neither he nor the panelists can make visible use of notes. Audible remarks to members by the moderator must usually take the place of such signals.

Finally, the seating arrangement is not always favorable to group discussion. Members of the group rarely can be seated around a table, as some of them would have their backs to the camera. And yet every attempt must be made to simulate a natural informal conversation such as might take place in one's living room. Sometimes moderator and members are seated in a shallow arc facing the camera; sometimes they are seated in the shape of a capital L, the moderator seated behind the short arm of the L and the panelists in a straight row behind the long arm. With such seating arrangements both moderator and panel members must take special care to keep the participation general and lively and to avoid allowing it to degenerate into a multiple interview in which the moderator addresses questions in turn to members who reply directly to him. To avoid this requires more care than in radio discussion.

While the difficulties that embarrass television discussion are serious, experience indicates that they can in large measure be overcome. In any case informal discussion programs are now more often broadcast for television than for radio reception.

Reference

Griffin, John A., "Round-Table Discussion on the Air," *Adult Education Bulletin,* vol. 5, June, 1941, p. 140.

CHAPTER 11

Discussion in the Classroom

According to one experienced teacher and counselor of teachers, "The highest of all teaching skills is that of *guiding group thinking.*"[1] Few educators would challenge the statement, though much classroom practice belies its acceptance.

The ability to stimulate and direct cooperative thinking deserves a high place among the teaching skills both for its difficulty and for its importance in the educational process. In no other phase of his work does the teacher need more sympathetic appreciation of the individual student's interests and needs or more complete objectivity in handling ideas; perhaps in no other is he called upon to be so deft and clearheaded. And yet it is in leading class discussion that he can most effectively stimulate independent thinking, inculcate standards of relevance and cogency, and develop habits of cooperative thought and action.

Those who advocate a wider use of discussion do not mean to imply that it is the only valid classroom procedure. The lecture is more effective in presenting a body of accepted fact or principle; and the methodical defense of an opinion or point of view either by the teacher or the student, is often useful. But when the

[1] W. H. Lancelot, *Handbook of Teaching Skills,* New York: John Wiley & Sons, Inc., 1929, p. 147.

132

object is to stimulate and clarify thinking, discussion is more effective than formal address.

Though widely accepted on theoretical grounds, the use of genuine discussion in the classroom is rare. This striking discrepancy between profession and practice may be due partly to the fact that much literature on discussion stresses the philosophy of group thinking without suggesting procedures for its application. Of necessity any teacher's equipment is in large part a collection of habitual practices. His accustomed methods, procedures, and devices, picked up from other teachers or devised by himself, are his stock in trade; without them he would be almost helpless. This may explain why it is often possible to convert a teacher to a new philosophy of education without effecting any noticeable change in his classroom practice. The teacher who adopts a new approach to his work must have a new set of habits.

The purpose of this chapter is to bridge the gap between the philosophy and practice of discussion by suggesting specific procedures for use in the classroom. For illustrative purposes suggestions will be couched in terms directly applicable to the four courses in which discussion seems especially appropriate—social studies, history, speech, and English—but a resourceful teacher can adapt many of the methods to other courses or to such extracurricular activities as assembly programs and student-council meetings.

Method in Classroom Discussion

In classes numbering no more than twenty, round-table discussion involving the entire class is effective. In a larger group it is less so; either discussion degenerates into the conventional recitation, or a few members do all of the talking while the rest listen. As most classes are too large for effective round-table discussion, a panel should usually be employed. In panel discussion a selected group of from four to six members, who have prepared themselves for the discussion, are seated in a semicircle facing the class. During the first two-thirds of the class period panel members discuss the question among themselves, after which other members of the class participate by expressing their own views or addressing questions to the panel. The program is conducted on the assumption that while members of the panel are chiefly responsible for previous study of the question, all members of the class hope to make up their minds on it.

As in all group thinking, the seating arrangement is important. Unfortunately the arrangement in many classrooms is both unsatisfactory and difficult to change. For round-table discussion members of the class should be seated around a large table or around the outside of a square formed by placing several small tables together. Where this is impracticable, they may be seated in one or more rows of chairs arranged in a semicircle. If the classroom is furnished with chairs or benches arranged in straight rows and permanently fixed to the floor, a strenuous effort should be made to find a more suitable meeting place. When a panel method is employed, the panel should be seated around a small table or in a semicircle facing the class.

Whether round-table or panel discussion is used, the teacher usually should serve as moderator. The quality of discussion depends so much on the moderator's skill that a succession of inept student leaders soon destroys confidence in the method. Some students can learn to lead discussion well, and those with aptitude should have an opportunity to develop their skill; but to have members of a class take turns in the moderator's chair jeopardizes the success of a program. Nearly all, however, can learn to participate effectively if the discussion is skillfully led.

A program of discussion in the classroom is more likely to succeed if the teacher explains in advance what is expected of participants. An informal talk on the nature and purpose of group thinking, on the attitudes favorable to effective participation, and on the importance of developing good discussion habits will do much to ensure the success of classroom discussion.

Classroom Projects

IN SOCIAL STUDIES. Perhaps more than any other part of the curriculum the course in social studies invites use of the discussion method. Dealing with sharply controversial issues, it affords a unique opportunity to develop appreciation of the distinction between fact and opinion, to cultivate a tolerant and cooperative attitude toward those of opposing views, and to impress upon the student the importance of his responsibility as a citizen. And it is in achieving precisely these objectives that group thinking is most useful. Many of the textbooks in social studies, too, are well adapted to use in connection with discussion. One, for example,[2] devotes a chapter to each of the main problem areas in American democracy and in each chapter proposes a controversial question for discussion, presents an impartial statement of fact on it, lists the principal arguments pro and con, and suggests references for further reading.

We will suppose that a class of twenty-five high school seniors using such a textbook has reached the chapter on immigration. When the class has read the chapter, one or two days are devoted to recitation and to round-table discussion addressed to the following questions: On what topics connected with immigration do we need further information? On what specific problems do we wish to make up our minds? In answer to the first question the class decides to hear a ten-minute informational report on each of the following topics: Our "Statue of Liberty" tradition as expressed in official documents and the utterances of national leaders; the history of immigration to this country; the history of our immigration laws; an analysis of our present population in terms of religion, race, and national origin; the existence in America of discrimination against minority groups. The teacher appoints five members of the class to prepare oral reports, perhaps suggesting references for further reading on each topic.

In answer to the second question, the class decides that after it has heard the reports it will devote one class period to considering each of the following controversial questions: How have our immigrants affected American life? Should racial, religious, and national groups attempt to preserve their identity in America? How can discrimination against such groups be most effec-

[2] John T. Greenan and Albert B. Meredith, *Everyday Problems of American Democracy*, Boston: Houghton Mifflin Company, 1938.

tively combated? What should be our future immigration policy? For discussion of each question the teacher appoints a panel of five members of the class representing at least some initial difference of opinion, suggests references for further reading, and arranges a meeting of each panel outside of class to work out an agenda for use in discussion.

Each member of the class now has an assignment that will occupy him for several days. In class two periods are devoted to hearing informational reports, each report being followed by a question period during which class members may probe the speaker for further information. If not satisfied with a report, the class may request the speaker to do further reading and bring in a supplementary report. In any case the speakers are expected to continue with their reading and to serve as resource persons during the panel discussions to follow.

When the reports have been heard, five days are devoted to panel discussion. On the third day of discussion, for example, one of the panels and the teacher, who is to serve as moderator, are seated around a small table facing the class. The question to be discussed has been phrased as follows: How can discrimination against minority groups be most effectively combated? The moderator states the question and presents the following agenda, which he has written on the blackboard:

1. Can the problem be solved by legislation?
2. Would an educational program in the public schools help?
3. What should each of us do when he encounters members of minority groups in
   a. School?
   b. Recreational activities?
   c. Social life?

During discussion the panel occasionally turns to one of the resource persons for additional information. As it completes its consideration of each major issue in the agenda, other members of the class are invited to participate for a few minutes by expressing their own views or addressing questions to panel members. At the session's close the moderator sums up the discussion.

One class period often seems inadequate for discussion of a controversial question, and if the schedule permits, more than one day may be devoted to some questions.

When the panel discussions have been completed, a final class period of round-table discussion is devoted to summarizing the two weeks' work on immigration.

IN HISTORY. The class in American history follows a similar pattern. When the class has studied the textbook chapters dealing with the American Civil War, for example, and has devoted several days to recitation, the following question is suggested for round-table discussion: On what problems connected with the Civil War would we like to make up our minds? After discussion the class decides to hear panel discussion of the following questions: Was the Civil War unavoidable? Is agitation like that conducted by the abolitionists desirable? Have subsequent events justified Lincoln's emancipation of the slaves? What should have been the national policy toward the South after the Civil War?

For each question the teacher appoints a panel of five or six students to do further reading, to prepare an agenda, and to present a panel discussion.

At least one day is devoted to each of the controversial questions. As each panel concludes its discussion, the rest of the class is invited to participate by presenting argument or addressing questions to panel members. Each member of the class not assigned to a panel also prepares a paper on one of the questions, in which he presents a reasoned defense of the answer he would make to the question.

IN SPEECH. Unless the course in speech must be restricted to training in public speaking, it should include study and practice in group discussion. Important as it may be that the student acquire skill in the preparation and delivery of speeches, it is no less important that he be effective in informal discussion. As a matter of fact, after leaving school he will more often participate in group discussion in a committee room than deliver public addresses from a platform. The teacher should present some of the material contained in earlier chapters of this book and arrange a series of round-table or panel discussions, followed by critical comment and suggestion on each student's performance.

Even if the course deals only with public speaking, some use of discussion will help to motivate the student speaker and guide him in preparation of his speech. If four or five students are interested in international control of atomic energy, they may present a panel discussion of the topic, inviting the class to intervene at convenient points with question and comment. Several days later the same students appear in a debate or symposium on the subject, each defending his own view. The clash of argument at close quarters in informal discussion has stimulated the student speaker's thinking, familiarized him in detail with views opposed to his own, and informed him in advance where other members of the class stand on the question. In consequence he is likely to plan his speech more intelligently and to deliver it more effectively.

IN ENGLISH. In courses dealing with literature and English composition discussion may seem less useful. Yet here also it will often motivate the student and stimulate and clarify his thinking. Writing on controversial topics—and these are not confined to politics and economics—displays more energy and more sense of purpose and direction when prompted by a lively discussion. An informal exchange of views stimulates the impulse to communicate and encourages the writer to feel that he has an audience and is operating in a real situation.

In the study of literature, too, discussion serves a purpose. If the class has just finished reading *David Copperfield*, it will enjoy a series of discussions on such questions as these: Are the characters in the novel fully motivated? Is the novel significant chiefly as a social document or as a work of literary art? How does the England of Dickens compare with the America we know? Such discussion prompts independent thinking, while a series of lectures from the teacher's desk may produce apathy or even an active dislike for a book which, properly taught, would give the student an interesting and stimulating experience. Out of the discussion may grow a thoughtful essay in which the student presents at length his own appraisal of the book.

So with the study of poetry. *The Rime of the Ancient Mariner,* when taught line by line, stanza by stanza, becomes a dreary conglomeration of iambics and ballad meters. Enlivened by classroom discussion of Coleridgean symbols and their larger significance, led by a teacher adept in the discussion method and aware of the meaning of the poem, the beauty and universality of an English masterpiece may so emerge as to become a permanent possession of the student rather than merely one more assignment to be finished and forgotten.

Many classics, when discussed informally by teacher and students after careful reading, may come to life for boys and girls, who by sharing one another's views make great books their own heritage.

The Teacher as Moderator

It is assumed in this chapter that the teacher who leads class discussion will equip himself with the methods recommended in earlier chapters. When moderating class discussion, he will need all of the skill he can develop. Our purpose here is not to emphasize that need, but to raise a more fundamental question: How can the teacher be a strictly impartial moderator without abandoning his role as teacher? Is not the teacher expected to impart knowledge and to inculcate certain attitudes universally accepted as desirable? How can he discharge this responsibility if he must remain impartial while leading discussion? The issue is too real to be brushed aside lightly.

The problem is encountered in the discussion of any controversial issue in the classroom, and such issues are not confined to the realm of public affairs; they arise in any area where difference of opinion occurs. While moderating discussion, the teacher may feel that the class, or panel, is arriving at erroneous conclusions based largely on ignorance or prejudice. Fortunately he can do much to remedy this situation without abandoning his role as moderator. In appointing members of the class to a panel he should take care that all points of view are represented, even though some of them are unpopular with the class as a whole. And while leading discussion he may properly call attention to facts that are being ignored or to arguments that are receiving less attention than they deserve. This he can do without becoming a party to the argument or expressing a preference for any particular conclusion. He is acting not as a custodian of truth, but as an exponent of sound method in thinking.

But in spite of such direction from the moderator's chair, may not the class arrive at what the teacher regards as an erroneous conclusion? It certainly may. But by definition a controversial topic is one on which the truth is not definitely known, and the teacher himself may be the one in error. In any case the teacher should be concerned primarily with *how* his students think rather than with *what* they think. To dictate what the class shall think on a controversial question is to regard the student as a means to an end, and it is a cardinal principle of education that the student himself is the end of the teacher's endeavor.

Suppose, however, that at the close of a discussion students turn to the teacher with the question, "What do *you* think?" In response to such a question there certainly can be no objection to the teacher's expressing his own views, provided he does not attempt to impose them on the class.

A somewhat different problem arises when the teacher employs discussion in areas that he does not regard as controversial. He should of course remember that what is not controversial today may become so tomorrow. Nevertheless there is a large body of what, for the present at least, the world has agreed to call accepted fact. To take an extreme example, the solution of quadratic equations by means of the quadratic formula is not a subject of controversy among those who understand quadratic equations. In history, too—though here we are on less solid ground—many facts can be regarded as established. Group discussion of such matters serves no useful purpose in the classroom or outside of it.

Yet to recognize that the discussion method is not applicable in the realm of established fact does not quite solve the problem.

Between the areas of the controversial and the noncontroversial lies a shadowy zone of principles, attitudes, and value judgments whose truth cannot be demonstrated but which our age, our civilization, or our nation regards as established. We sometimes speak of this body of material as our cultural heritage, and we understand it to be one of the teacher's functions to pass it on to future generations. Thus we expect him to inculcate the principles of democracy on his students and to teach them the virtues of tolerance and respect for others. But we are now on somewhat difficult ground if we advise the teacher that the discussion method is applicable in this area. A class discussion may reach the conclusion that dictatorship is preferable to democracy or that discrimination against racial minorities is desirable.

One possible solution may be suggested by anyone familiar with the discussion method. Is it not sometimes possible for a skillful moderator to steer discussion toward a predetermined "sound" conclusion without appearing to do so? It is. By throwing out a series of carefully prepared questions to provoke discussion and then by elaborating upon the favorable responses and ignoring the unfavorable, a moderator can sometimes bring a group to a desired conclusion without any member's suspecting that the thinking of the group has been manipulated for an ulterior purpose. But however good the purpose, the method must be condemned. It is a perversion of group thinking and in the end is self-defeating. Those whose responses were ignored have not really been convinced, and the more observant will eventually detect the advocate behind the teacher's mask of simulated impartiality.

In the long run it is sounder to regard as frankly controversial any matter upon which difference of opinion actually exists. As a matter of fact, no belief is so widely held or so deeply cherished that it is not being challenged by someone somewhere; and if students do not know this now, the sooner they learn it the better. Nor should we regret the tendency of young people to examine traditional beliefs critically; each generation must do its own thinking. It is comforting to reflect that insofar as traditional belief is sound, it will survive critical examination; for free discussion is a better preservative of truth than indoctrination.

References

Junior Town Meeting League, 356 Washington Street, Middletown, Connecticut, four pamphlets: *Discussion and Current Affairs; Make Youth Discussion Conscious; Teaching Controversial Issues; Learning Through Group Discussion.*

Maaske, Roben J., "Using the Panel Discussion Method in High School Teaching," *High School Journal,* vol. 21 (February, 1938), pp. 44-48, 72.

Our Times, a weekly newspaper for schools, American Education Publications, 1250 Fairwood Avenue, Columbus 16, Ohio.

CHAPTER 12

The Business Conference

Traditionally, commercial and industrial firms, like units of the armed forces, have been organized on the authoritarian principle. The president of a firm, responsible only to a board of directors, is the sole source of authority within an organization. He delegates authority and responsibility to his immediate subordinates, the major executives of the firm, who in turn delegate it to their own subordinates, and so on down the line of command to the individual employee. The power to formulate policy, though divided among members of the administrative hierarchy, is vested in individuals, not in groups. Under this arrangement group thinking has no place in the administrative process. While an executive may summon his staff to a meeting for the purpose of making announcements, issuing orders, or explaining directives, he does not invite them to participate collectively in the formulation of policy.

In practice probably no industrial firm operates exclusively on the line-of-command principle; at all administrative levels executives occasionally seek the advice of subordinates in deciding a difficult question of policy. But conference for this purpose can hardly be regarded as typical of the administrative process in most industrial organizations.

In the business world generally, however, a more democratic conception of the administrative process is finding increasing favor among practical administrators. According to the new view, the functions of formulating and executing policy should not be sharply divorced; when the staff which is to carry out a policy has a hand in its formulation, the policy is often more soundly conceived and more effectively executed. Group responsibility for formulation of policy discourages private griping, develops pride in the organization, and, in accomplishing these ends, makes every member of the organization from vice-president to machinist an effective public relations officer of the firm. These are important advantages. Against them must be set the undeniable fact that group thinking consumes more time than decision by one person. Often the necessary time is not available. While the line-of-command conception is unlikely to disappear from industrial management, it is apparently giving ground to a more democratic conception of administration.

Types of Conference

If a conference is regarded as any meeting at which several persons are invited to think together, it is clear that the business conference may serve many purposes. In the practice of some industrial and commercial firms it will be found serving at least the following ends: to exchange information, to train employees, to advise superior officers on questions of policy, to formulate policy, and to adjust differences between two or more groups within an organization.

The conference to exchange information does not attempt to reach agreement on the solution of a problem. Its purpose rather is to pool information and experience for such use as the individual conferees may care to make of it. The foremen in a plant, for example, may meet to share their experience on a problem that all encounter in their work, perhaps that of accident prevention or the maintenance of morale. No attempt is made to agree on a uniform policy, but each conferee hopes to profit from the experience of his colleagues.

In purpose and method the conference to exchange information has much in common with the training conference, which has been widely used for many years to provide in-service training for certain types of experienced employees. The sales force of an insurance company, for example, may be called in to the central office to devote several days to discussion of method in selling. A group of ten or twelve salesmen may represent an aggregate of a hundred years of experience in the field; often they can learn more from each other than from an expert on salesmanship. Typical problems encountered in the field are analyzed, and an attempt is made to work out cooperatively the principles and procedures most effective in dealing with them. In some cases the conclusions reached are embodied in directives issued to the sales force; in others each salesman is free to pick and choose from among the recommendations growing out of discussion. The training conference is applicable to any group of employees who are engaged in the same type of work and have enough knowledge and experience to contribute to group thinking.

Any executive occasionally seeks advice on questions of policy from individual members of his staff. Less frequently he calls a staff meeting to discuss a problem and work out cooperatively a set of recommendations for his consideration. An excellent example of the systematic use of an advisory conference is the Junior Board set up in 1932 by President Charles P. McCormick, of McCormick and Company, Baltimore, and subsequently established in some five hundred other business organizations. The Junior Board is composed of promising junior executives from all departments of the organization who meet regularly to consider problems of policy and to formulate recommendations for consideration in the front office. It is understood that the board's powers are advisory only but that any proposal backed by its unanimous recommendation will receive careful consideration by the appropriate senior executive.

The potential values of group thinking are of course more fully realized when a group is entrusted with power to formulate policy rather than merely to advise a superior officer. It is not always feasible for an executive, who will be held personally responsible for the result, to delegate policy-making power to a staff of subordinates. Yet, increasingly, executives are finding it both feasible and desirable. Often the power must be exercised under carefully defined limitations. A department manager, for example, may call together his staff of junior executives and say, "I am turning over to you the problem of revising our departmental policy on the use of our stenographic and secretarial staff. If you can reach agreement, I will follow your recommendations. But note that no policy is acceptable that would increase the department's payroll or violate our contract with the union."

A group charged with the responsibility of solving a problem of policy will sometimes find that no solution is possible without the cooperation of other departments of the organization. The foreman of a shop, requested by his supervisor to clear floor space by prompter removal of a finished product, may find no solution within the shop itself. The pressure of other shops on the plant's transportation system may be such that this particular shop can expect no relief unless transportation services are expanded or reallocated. Clearly the situation calls for a conference between the transportation manager and the supervisors of the various shops within the plant. In any large organization employing democratic procedures the intergroup conference plays an important role.

Conditions of Profitable Discussion

The conditions of profitable discussion enumerated in Chapter 2 are as essential to success in the business conference as in any other form of group thinking. But in a busy plant or office it is not always easy to provide favorable conditions. Often a special effort must be made at this point if the conference method is to succeed.

The group invited to confer should be made up of those who are concerned with the problem to be discussed, who will be expected to carry out any policy adopted, or who will be affected by the policy. And they should be persons of sufficient knowledge and experience to make a real contribution to discussion. Unless so constituted, the group will attach little importance to the business before it; for it will feel either that no problem exists or that it is incapable of solving it. In other words, the constitution of a group has much to do with its motivation.

Other factors also affect motivation. Prominent among them is the relationship existing between superior and subordinate members of an organization. An attitude of hostility, fear, or suspicion on the part of a subordinate or of arrogance or intolerance on the part of a superior makes good discussion impossible, especially when both are seated at the same conference table. If a group does not understand whether it is empowered to formulate policy or only to offer advice, or if in the past its recommendations have apparently been ignored in the front office, it will attach little importance to its conference work. Poor motivation also results from holding perfunctory meetings at which no important problem is presented for discussion.

The size of a group is an important factor in the successful conference. It may sometimes be as small as three or four or as large as twenty. Twelve to fifteen is perhaps the ideal number. A very small group usually does not represent a sufficient diversity of background and viewpoint for profitable discussion, and a very large one cannot confer informally.

The ideal conference room is just large enough to seat the group comfortably, preferably around a large rectangular table. It contains a portable blackboard and wall space for display of charts and maps; it is well lighted and comfortably heated; it is free from intrusion of persons not attending the conference and from such distracting noises as the sound of machinery and the clatter of typewriters. Unfortunately, the ideal room is seldom available. In many cases it is necessary to confer in the office of a member, usually that of the executive who is calling the conference. When such an office must be used, precautions should be taken to reduce interruptions to a minimum by having a secretary screen visitors and reroute all but the most urgent telephone calls. If at all possible, a special conference room should be provided.

Occasionally a group may find it possible and desirable to meet outside of working hours, but most conferences are held on company time. This is perhaps just as well. It impresses upon conferees the importance attached by the organization to conference work. The conference should be set at an hour that will occasion least inconvenience to those attending; it should seldom last longer than an hour and a half; it should open and close promptly.

It is the conference leader's responsibility to arrange in advance for the presentation of any information the conference may need in its work. He may prepare maps, charts, or diagrams for wall display, arrange exhibits for use in demonstration, prepare printed or typed copies of statistical material, or invite outside persons to attend for the purpose of supplying information. Of necessity, most conferences involve a considerable investment of time. None of it should be wasted in idle speculation because the necessary information has not been made available; nor should the conference mark time while someone goes upstairs to find material that should have been at hand.

As in all forms of group thinking, selection of the right man to lead a discussion is of vital importance. On this point nothing need be added here to the suggestions made in Chapter 6 except in regard to the situation arising in a business conference when the discussion leader is also the superior officer of those attending the conference. He often will be. It is natural, for example, for a staff conference of junior executives to be conducted by the department head. Unfortunately a senior executive is not always a good discussion leader. He may have reached his present position in the organization through technical competence in a specialized field rather than through skill in working with groups and may have little aptitude, training, or experience in moderating discussion. Even when he has the necessary qualifications for leadership, some difficulty may arise from the very fact that he is the boss.

Little genuine group thinking will occur unless a superior officer lays aside the mantle of authority while in the moderator's chair. Those seated at the table must speak frankly if the conference is to succeed, and they will not do so unless convinced that the boss can "take it." The leader should discourage apple polishing and give respectful and sympathetic attention to any contribution made. Some executives need to learn that the conference leader must be, first of all, a good listener rather than a voluminous talker. Usually, he must avoid expressing his own opinion if he really wishes to know what his subordinates think.

Sometimes a qualified member from another department of the organization can be invited to lead discussion. Among any group of executives there will be some with a flair for this type of work. The personnel director, for example, is likely to be well qualified for it. The fact that he is not an expert on the problem to be discussed does not disqualify him provided the discussion is not too technical for him to follow. Such a guest moderator probably should be at least the equal in organizational rank of those attending the conference.

An organization wishing to make considerable use of the conference method would do well to set up a training program for those who are expected to lead discussion. This is one point at which a reasonable degree of skill is necessary for satisfactory results.

Planning the Conference

In following the suggestions contained in Chapter 6 the leader of discussion in a commercial or industrial organization may encounter several problems peculiar to a business setting. One concerns the leader's preparation for a conference.

That he must usually prepare and prepare carefully should go without saying; probably more business conferences fail through poor preparation than for any other reason. We have already noted the leader's responsibility to make arrangements in advance for presentation of information that may be needed in discussion. What further planning should he do?

To be useful, discussion must usually be methodical; that is, it must follow a plan worked out in advance by the leader. This does not imply that the leader knows what conclusions the group will reach; still less does it imply that he steers discussion toward predetermined conclusions. His plan of the conference consists not of conclusions to be agreed upon, but of steps to be taken in discussion or of questions to be raised and answered.

In Chapter 4 it was suggested that before a group launches

into discussion of proposed solutions of a problem, it should devote some time to an analysis of the problem and the preparation of an agenda. During this preliminary discussion the group will often consider these questions:

1. What is the problem to be solved?
2. Out of what facts does it arise?
3. What objectives do we wish to achieve in solving it?
4. What specific solutions should we examine?

Having explored these matters, the group sets up an agenda, or list of questions, indicating the issues to be discussed in detail.

Chapter 4 may have seemed to imply that this period of preliminary discussion culminating in the framing of an agenda is usually brief and that sometimes a leader himself can do the preliminary thinking and prepare an agenda for a group. This is often true when a group is to consider a question of public policy that has already been under discussion. It is less true of a business conference, where often one cannot assume general understanding or agreement regarding what the problem is, what facts surround it, what objectives are to be achieved in solving it, or what solutions ought to be examined. A conference may need to spend a good deal of time in clearing up these matters before attempting to appraise solutions. It is seldom, therefore, that a leader can work out a detailed agenda in advance. Often his conference plan will indicate steps to be taken in discussion rather than detailed questions to be answered.

As the nature of a plan depends a good deal on the purpose of the conference and the circumstances surrounding it, a leader needs principles rather than rules of thumb to guide him. Let us consider the planning of several typical conferences.

Six foremen in a shop have agreed to meet in a series of conferences to exchange information about their work. At the first meeting they intend only to survey the ground and select four or five problems for detailed examination at future meetings. Little planning need be done for the first meeting. After a few introductory remarks the leader raises the question, What difficulties do you encounter in your work? As members of the conference suggest difficulties, the leader writes them on a blackboard. After a brief consideration of each the group selects four or five that have been found especially perplexing by nearly all of those present, and agreement is reached regarding the order in which they will be considered at future meetings.

We will suppose that at the second session the group will exchange information on the problem of accident prevention. Both the nature of the problem and the objective to be attained are already clear and will require no discussion. What remedies will be proposed and what objections will be raised to each the leader cannot foresee. His plan of the conference, of necessity a simple one, may take the following form:

1. Brief introductory statement by the leader on the plant's accident record.
2. Questions for discussion:
   a. What is the accident situation in your part of the shop?
   b. What are the underlying causes of accidents in that shop?
   c. What remedies have you tried and with what results?
   d. What new remedies would you propose?
3. Summary of discussion.

Let us now suppose that a training conference for salesmen is to devote one of a series of sessions to the problem of how to approach a difficult prospect. At the preceding sessions it was agreed that the hostile prospect, the busy prospect, and the uninterested prospect present especially baffling problems. The leader has arranged to have each problem presented in a five-minute dramatic skit in which prospect and salesman are impersonated by members of the conference. At this conference members hope to get beyond the mere exchange of information and to reach agreement on how best to approach each type of prospect. The leader's plan may take the following form:

1. Introductory remarks by the leader.
2. Dramatic presentation of each problem:
   a. The hostile prospect,

      b. The busy prospect,

      c. The uninterested prospect.

3. Questions for discussion of each problem:
   a. Why did the prospect react as he did?
   b. Could his reaction have been foreseen?
   c. How should he have been approached?
4. Summary of conclusions regarding methods to be followed in approaching each type of prospect.

Let us turn now to a conference that has been authorized to formulate a policy—a policy, let us say, regarding use of the secretarial staff in an office. Under the existing office arrangement one secretary is assigned to the manager of a department; the others make up a pool on which any junior executive can draw when in need of secretarial help. Several men in the office have asked that a secretary be assigned to each of them permanently to take dictation and keep their files in order.

This conference differs in several respects from those described above. The conference is to solve a problem and formulate a policy which, if substantial agreement is reached, will be put into effect at once. The possible solution—that already requested by several of the men—is known in advance. The leader's plan for the conference might take the following form:

  I. Statement of the problem by the leader.

 II. Questions for discussion:
    A. In what way is the present situation unsatisfactory?
    B. By what objectives are we to weigh the proposed policy?
      1. To increase the efficiency with which each executive's secretarial work is done?
      2. To ensure that each executive will have the services of a secretary when he needs them?
      3. To ensure that all of the secretaries are kept busy?
    C. Would the proposed plan accomplish these objectives more fully than the present plan?
    D. Would a combination of the present and the proposed plan achieve the objectives more fully than either plan alone?

III. Summary of conclusions reached.
IV. (If a change in policy has been agreed upon.) What steps must be taken to put the new policy into effect?

An intergroup conference called to adjust an apparent conflict of interest between two or more departments of an organization does not present a problem essentially different from that posed by the intradepartmental conference. We may suppose that the supervisor of a shop in a plant has complained that the finished product is not removed promptly from his shop, and the transportation manager has been unwilling, or unable, to provide more adequate transportation services. One of the major executives has called into conference the transportation manager and the supervisors of the shops served by the transportation system. The leader's plan for the conference might run about as follows:

1. Statement of the problem by the leader.
2. Statement by the complaining supervisor, the transportation manager, and others of the causes of the problem.
3. Consideration of the objectives to be achieved by any solution adopted.
4. Consideration of changes in the present policy in the light of the facts and the objectives agreed upon.
5. Summary of conclusions reached.
6. Consideration of steps to be taken to translate the conclusions into action.

In all of these situations the leader's conference plan, though a simple one, serves the important purpose of ensuring that in its discussion the group will follow an orderly sequence of steps in its search for a solution. Typically the steps are as follows:

1. Statement of the problem.
2. Statement of the facts.
3. Consideration of objectives.
4. Examination of proposals in the light of the facts and objectives agreed upon.
5. Summary of the discussion.
6. Consideration of means to implement the decision.

The Labor–Management Conference

The negotiation of wage contracts by representatives of labor and management would be greatly facilitated by more of the spirit and method of group thinking. Occasionally, and increasingly, cooperative thinking does occur at the labor–management conference table; but it can hardly be considered typical of the procedures employed there.

While the advantages of cooperation in this phase of industrial life are obvious, the atmosphere in which wage negotiations are conducted is often unfavorable to group thinking. Those seated at the table are spokesmen for powerful groups not present and are, therefore, not entirely free agents. Often the interests of the two parties are, or are thought to be, in irreconcilable conflict. Back of the discussion lurks the threat of an appeal to force through a strike or lockout. And the method of conducting negotiations is sometimes unfortunate. Labor representatives talk in terms of "demands," which management may "deny" or "grant." On both sides the attitude and intent implied in the phraseology used is inimical to cooperative thinking. In view of these difficulties it is not surprising that wage negotiation often achieves nothing more satisfactory than a compromise which both parties accept reluctantly.

It would be idle to expect a radical change overnight in the method of negotiating contracts. The difficulties that embarrass negotiation are too real and too difficult to circumvent easily. Yet labor and management do have a substantial interest in common—the desire to avoid interruption of production. And in many cases they do think of themselves as partners in an industrial enterprise and conduct negotiations in a commendable spirit of cooperation.

While it is never easy to develop in a labor-management conference the mutual confidence and cooperative spirit necessary for group thinking, some conditions and methods are more likely than others to create the desired atmosphere.

To begin with, it is essential that a moderator be strictly impartial and acceptable to both parties. No cooperative thinking is possible if anyone at the table regards the leader as a party to the argument. This will often necessitate calling in a moderator from outside an organization, though occasionally some member of the managerial staff has such a reputation for fairness and impartiality that he is acceptable to both sides.

Both parties should have the same number of representatives at a conference table, and conferees should be so seated as to break up labor and management groups. When union leader and management representative rub elbows, there is somewhat less danger that a conference will polarize immediately into two hostile factions.

Many conferences get off to a bad start with a formal statement of "demands" by the union and a counterstatement by management of the maximum "concessions" it is willing to make. After this opening nothing further is possible but a process of horse trading looking toward eventual compromise. More thinking will be done if each party presents, first, a factual statement of the situation as he sees it. The accuracy and relevance of a statement of fact can be examined more disinterestedly before it has been used to buttress argument. Preliminary discussion of facts will also sometimes remove misunderstanding and reveal more common ground of agreement than was at first suspected.

It may also be desirable, after examining the facts and before considering proposals, to discuss the objectives (in terms of such factors as standard of living and rate of profit) that ought to be realized by a new contract. Here, too, there is more likelihood of finding common ground of agreement if concrete proposals and counterproposals have not yet been presented.

Each party should now be invited to present a proposal based on the previous discussion of facts and objectives. No attempt should be made to argue the merits of these proposals until both are thoroughly understood. Then the conference should proceed, first, to discussion of the points covered in both proposals, noting the points of agreement, if any, and threshing out one at a time the points of disagreement. Later, attention should be turned to points covered in one proposal but not in the other.

In making the foregoing suggestions in the interest of a more cooperative approach to a negotiation of contracts, we do not mean to imply that a labor–management conference can always employ successfully the methods of group thinking. Under present conditions in industry an element of force, or a threat of force, is probably unavoidable. But a wage conference need not always be, as it so often is, a naked contest of power.

The prospects of cooperative thinking in the negotiation of contracts will be brighter when both labor and management more often select their representatives with a view to their skill in conference and especially when both provide their representatives with training for this difficult and important work.

References

Busch, Henry M., *Conference Methods in Industry,* New York: Harper & Row, Publishers, 1949.

Chamberlain, Neil W., "Group Discussion and Collective Bargaining," *Adult Education Bulletin,* XIII, no. 3 (February, 1949), p. 77.

Cooper, Alfred M., *How To Conduct Conferences,* New York: McGraw-Hill Book Co., Inc., 1946.

Executive Leadership: Conference Leader's Manual, Bureau of Business Practice, National Foremen's Institute, Inc., Deep River, Connecticut, 1940.

Hannaford, Earle S., *Conference Leadership in Business and Industry,* New York: McGraw-Hill Book Co., Inc., 1945.

Heyel, Carl, *Standard Business Conference Technique,* New York: Funk & Wagnalls Co., Inc., 1948.

McCormick, Charles P., *The Power of People,* New York: Harper & Row, Publishers, 1949.

Maier, Norman R. F., *Problem-solving Discussions and Conferences,* New York: McGraw-Hill Book Co., Inc., 1963.

Taylor, George W., "The Labor-Management Conference as an Aid to Collective Bargaining," *The Annals of the American Academy of Political and Social Science,* vol. 250 (March, 1947), pp. 53-59.

Tead, Ordway, *The Art of Leadership,* New York: McGraw-Hill Book Co., Inc., 1935, Chap. 10.

CHAPTER 13

The Large Discussion Conference

The nature of group thinking imposes one inconvenient limitation on its use—it can be employed only in a small group. Yet in many situations it is desirable for a large number to participate cooperatively in the formulation of policy. A representative group of several hundred—or even several thousand—clergymen and laymen, for example, may wish to determine the attitude to be taken by the church on a current social problem; or several hundred representatives of labor, management, and government may wish to explore together the problems of industrial relations. The area in which group thinking by large numbers may be profitable is probably growing as our society becomes more complex; for increasingly many persons are affected by policy and can contribute usefully to its formulation.

As a matter of fact cooperative thinking often is employed by large groups in what we shall call the *discussion conference*. Such a conference is a gathering of from fifty to a thousand persons who devote several days, or weeks, to the consideration of a common problem and conduct their deliberations by informal discussion rather than by parliamentary debate. Meetings of this kind have become a familiar institution. We read daily of conferences of youth groups, of churchmen, of economists, of educators, of scientists, of industrialists, of labor leaders, of government officials. Not all of these groups employ informal discussion exclusively; but many do, and the practice of substituting discussion for debate is growing. The discussion conference sometimes aims only at the exchange of information, as when city managers meet to learn of each other's problems and methods. More often it seeks to solve a problem, to resolve a conflict, or to formulate a policy. In the case of youth and religious groups its purpose often is educational.

While the preparation and conduct of a successful discussion conference requires careful planning and a good deal of administrative work, the purely administrative problems are not formidable. Nor is there any difficulty in providing for informal discussion by dividing a conference into small groups of fifteen or twenty each for simultaneous round-table sessions. The real difficulty is in synthesizing results of the various round-table discussions in a set of conclusions reflecting a consensus of the entire group. To do this effectively requires special procedures, but the methods are available and experience has repeatedly demonstrated their value.

The methods employed in a discussion conference depend somewhat on the purpose of the meeting and the number of those attending. They depend also on whether all of the small groups into which the conference is organized are to discuss the entire problem or are to divide the problem among them, each discussing one portion only. Certain procedures, however, are common to all conferences at which the discussion method is employed. In the following pages we shall examine the difficulties most often encountered and suggest some of the means employed to overcome them, assuming for the purpose of explanation that the conference is one in which all of the smaller groups discuss the entire problem. This general discussion will then be illustrated by a somewhat detailed account of an actual conference held a few years ago in Ohio.

Organization

It is sometimes supposed that informal discussion dispenses with organization and division of labor, that it does not need a mind to direct it or eyes, ears, hands, and feet to serve it. This is a capital mistake. Without organization group thinking is especially liable to confusion and futility. A set of officials must be provided to direct and serve the conference, and the membership must be organized into small groups capable of cooperative deliberation.

Over-all direction of a conference should be entrusted to a director well qualified for his work by training or experience. In planning the conference he should have the active assistance of a conference committee representative of the persons or groups who are to attend, which can meet with him regularly before the conference and be available for special meetings while it is in session. In preparing the conference, the director and committee will need to appoint at least the following officials: a moderator to lead each round table, a recorder for each round table to prepare brief reports of the conclusions reached in each session, resource persons to supply information to the conference, secretaries to type up reports and take care of administrative detail, and pages to carry messages from one part of the conference to another.

The conferees must be organized in advance into small groups for round-table discussion, the number in each usually not exceeding fifteen or twenty. It is important that each group represent a cross section of the interest, background, and opinion of the entire conference. In a large conference this may be accomplished by assigning members to round tables alphabetically or at random. Sometimes, however, it is possible and preferable to ascertain in advance about where each conferee stands on the question to be discussed and to make assignments ensuring a balance of viewpoint and opinion in each group. When members come to a conference as delegations representing local groups, it is wise to distribute the members of each delegation among the various round tables. Finally, experience indicates that the original division into small groups should remain fixed for duration of the conference. This gives the members of each round table an opportunity to become acquainted and to develop an *esprit de corps* favorable to good discussion.

Preparation

Much of the planning by a director and committee must be done before a conference assembles, and it is wise to estimate liberally the time required for this work.

PRELIMINARY ARRANGEMENTS. Early in planning decisions must be made, at least tentatively, regarding the probable size of the conference and the time schedule to be followed. When shall the conference be held? How long shall it last? About how many will attend? Into how many groups will they be divided for informal discussion? How many times will each group meet? How long shall these informal sessions be? How often and for what periods of time will the entire conference assemble in one room? Having reached tentative decisions on these matters, the committee must decide where and how to house the conference. In addition to an assembly hall capable of seating the entire group, it will be necessary to provide, for informal discussion, a sufficient number of small conference rooms conveniently situated and suitably equipped with large tables, chairs, and blackboards. In some cases provision must be made also for lodging and feeding conferees.

BRIEFING THE CONFEREES. Often another early task of the planning committee is to select and define the problem for discussion. Occasionally the problem is given, as when the president of a national organization summons state officials to consider an urgent question of organizational policy. And sometimes a conference meets to explore a problem area rather than to solve a specific problem, as when industrialists and labor leaders assemble to discuss industrial relations. In the first case previous selection of the problem is unnecessary; in the second it is impossible, and the task must be undertaken by the conference itself. But setting up the problem after the conference meets consumes valuable time and should be avoided whenever possible.

Usually those who are to confer know in advance the general

area within which discussion is to occur but have not agreed upon a specific problem. A national youth group, for example, may know only that it wishes to devote its annual meeting to some problem growing out of interracial relations. In selecting the specific problem the preferences of those who are to attend, or of the local groups that are to send delegates, should of course be consulted. To accomplish this the conference committee may invite group representatives to a preconference planning session, or it may send each participating group a questionnaire suggesting six or eight problems to be listed in the order of preference. When finally selected, the problem should be stated interrogatively.

It is sometimes desirable to supplement the statement of a problem with a definition of terms. This would certainly be true of the question: Should we press now for world federal government? To avoid confusion and misunderstanding *world federal government* should be defined in terms of some specific proposal, perhaps that advocated by the United World Federalists; or the committee should draft a brief statement indicating the type of world organization to be discussed.

When the tentative preliminary arrangements for a conference have been made and the problem has been selected and defined, this information should be sent to the persons or groups who are to attend. If the personnel of a conference is to be determined by responses to an invitation, invitations should accompany the announcement and those expecting to attend should be asked to reply promptly.

When it is known, from responses to invitations or otherwise, who is to attend, certain materials should go to the prospective conferees. In addition to a statement and definition of the question to be discussed, each should receive well in advance of the conference a statement of the agenda to be followed, bibliographies or reading material to be used in preparing for discussion, and a schedule of the principal events of the conference. Little can be expected from a conference at which the conferees arrive bewildered and unprepared.

BRIEFING THE OFFICIALS. Reference has already been made to the importance of selecting carefully the administrative staff, the moderators and recorders, and the resource persons who are to serve as consultants on the problem to be discussed. But careful selection of officials is not enough; each must be instructed in performance of his duties. Briefing the administrative staff and the recorders presents no difficulty; but if the moderators are without previous experience, they should be invited to a pre-conference training session. Upon their competence depends so largely the success of the conference that no pains should be spared in preparing them for their work.

The consultants, too, need some instruction. They should understand that they are appearing not as advocates, but as resource persons on whom the conference will rely for information. They should, therefore, be studiously impartial in making their contribution. If they are to speak only when summoned to appear before a round table to answer specific questions, this should be made clear to them. If they will be called upon to speak at greater length before the entire conference—perhaps to supply background material before the round tables take up a particular issue—this also should be made clear. In either case they should understand that their usefulness will depend very much upon their adaptability.

Procedure

As members of the conference arrive and report to conference headquarters for registration, each should be handed a copy of the schedule to be followed, indicating the hours at which general assemblies and round tables will meet, and should be referred to a bulletin board for assignment to a round table. The bulletin board should indicate also where each round table will meet and who will serve as moderator and recorder.

At the opening assembly, after an address of welcome and announcements, the director of the conference formally presents the problem for discussion, reviews the definition of terms, if any has been agreed upon in advance, and outlines the agenda to be followed. If background material is necessary for discussion of the first issue, one of the consultants is called upon to present it. The assembly then adjourns, and the round tables meet for discussion of the first issue.

As each round table, under the leadership of its moderator, examines the issue, the recorder takes notes on the discussion and at the end of the session writes out or dictates to a conference secretary a brief statement of the conclusions reached. When discussion runs aground for lack of information, the moderator sends a page stationed in the room to summon one of the consultants.

To synthesize the conclusions reached by the various round tables in a statement acceptable to the entire conference requires special procedures. In a conference not numbering more than a hundred the synthesis may be effected in a panel discussion held at the next assembly. Each round table sends to the platform its recorder or some other spokesman armed with the recorder's report, and the round-table representatives seat themselves in a semicircle facing the audience with a moderator at the center. After each spokesman has reported the findings of his round table, the points of disagreement are ironed out in informal discussion, some time being reserved for question and comment from the floor. At the close of discussion a recorder prepares a statement of the consensus of the conference on the issue under consideration.

At a larger conference this procedure will not be found satisfactory. Unless a public-address system is used, the audience will have difficulty in hearing the informal discussion on the platform; and in any case the process will consume too much total conference time. It is usually more satisfactory to allow time between each round of group discussion and the next assembly period for a private meeting of round-table spokesmen to compose their differences and prepare a report for presentation to the next assembly.

At the second assembly the consensus of the conference on the first issue is reported; the second issue is submitted for discussion; background material, if needed in discussion of the issue, is presented; and the conference again breaks up for informal discussion. This alternation of assembly periods and round-table discussion continues throughout the conference. If the conference lasts several days or longer, mimeographed copies of the conclusions reached on each issue may be made available as promptly as they can be prepared.

The final assembly closes with a report of the conclusions reached on the problem as a whole. And when appropriate provision is made, through the appointment of committees or otherwise, to translate conclusions into action.

If the conference is to be one of a series, provision should be made for evaluating its procedures, so that the planning committee of the second conference can profit from the mistakes of the first. The officials, the planning committee, and a selected group of the conferees may meet for this purpose at or near the close of the conference; or they may be asked to submit reports based on a questionnaire distributed at the final session. At some conferences a special committee on evaluation is appointed to visit the sessions and prepare a report for the use of the next planning committee.

A High School Discussion Conference

A few years ago a hundred students from high schools of central and southwestern Ohio met in Columbus for a two-day discussion conference.

For several months preceding the meeting the conference director had been developing plans with the assistance of a committee of teachers and students representing some of the interested schools. Arrangements were made to house the conference at University High School on The Ohio State University campus; a list was prepared of schools to be invited; it was decided that each participating school would send five student delegates; it was agreed to propose for discussion world federal government and to phrase the question as follows: Should we press now for world federal government? With these preliminary details arranged, the committee issued invitations to the high schools of central Ohio, stating the time and place of the meeting, the nature of the conference to be held, the question to be discussed, the size of the delegation to be sent by each school, and promising further information and assistance to those expecting to attend.

While awaiting replies to the invitation, the committee prepared for distribution to participating schools kits of materials including the following items: a definition of *world federal government*, the agenda to be followed in discussion, a bibliography on world government, and pamphlets containing informational and controversial material on the subject. The kit contained also a schedule of principal conference events and a three-page mimeographed statement on how to participate in discussion. This statement stressed the importance of a cooperative, noncontentious attitude, recommended the five "good discussion habits" discussed in Chapter 5 of this book, and advised each student to prepare for the conference by reading and discussion but to avoid committing himself to unalterable conclusions. To the high school teacher it was suggested that study and discussion of world government be included in the work of courses in speech, English, and social studies.

Two weeks before the date of the conference the committee requested schools to select their delegations and to have each student indicate whether at that time he was favorable to world government, opposed to it, or undecided about it. In connection with this request the committee made it clear that the expression of opinion did not commit any student to the view expressed, that on the contrary it was hoped he would avoid reaching fixed conclusions before arriving at the conference. On the basis of this tentative expression of opinion the committee divided the hundred students expecting to attend into ten round tables of ten each, taking care to break up school delegations and to ensure in each round table a cross section of preconference opinion.

Meanwhile final plans for the conference were being drawn. Provision was made for housing and feeding delegates; arrangements were completed for the use at University High School of a large assembly hall and ten small conference rooms; a conference secretary was instructed in her duties; a staff of pages was recruited from among the students of University High School; two members of the university's department of political science were appointed to serve as consultants on world government and instructed in their duties; a head moderator was appointed, who in turn recruited from a university course in discussion a staff of moderators to lead the round-table discussions. On the day before the conference each moderator received a copy of the following instructions:

Consult the bulletin board at Conference Headquarters for your assignment to a round table and for information regarding the times and places at which your round table will meet.

At the beginning of each round-table session select, or have the group elect, a member to serve as recorder. As the group completes its discussion of each main point raised during consideration of an issue, have the recorder write down the result in a terse sentence. On some points the group may have reached agreement; on others it may have failed to agree. The recorder's statement, which should not exceed five or six sentences in length, may need revising at the close of the session. It should state the group's position on each issue discussed during the hour. At the end of the session this statement is to be handed to the group's spokesman for use in the assembly period immediately following.

At the close of each session select, or have the group elect, a spokesman to represent it in the panel discussion at the assembly following the round-table discussion. The spokesman, who is to take to the platform the recorder's report from his group, should himself be effective in discussion and cooperative and objective enough to do justice in panel discussion to the various shades of opinion represented in his group.

If your group needs facts for the more intelligent consideration of a point, send the page stationed in your room to summon one of the consultants. He will supply the information desired and then withdraw.

Dismiss each round-table session on time, so the succeeding assembly period can start promptly.

As the conferees reported for registration on the morning of the conference, each was handed a copy of the schedule of events, was referred to the bulletin board for his assignment to a round table, and was asked to record his opinion on the question to be discussed on the following ballot:

OPINION POLL

Name: School: City:

At the beginning of the conference my attitude toward pressing now for world federal government is

_____Strongly favorable
_____Slightly favorable
_____Undecided
_____Slightly opposed
_____Strongly opposed

These ballots were filed for comparison later with a similar poll conducted at the close of the conference.

The printed schedule of events distributed at the registration desk was as follows:

HIGH SCHOOL DISCUSSION CONFERENCE

at

The University High School, Columbus, Ohio

QUESTION: Should we press now for world federal government?

CONFERENCE PROGRAM

FRIDAY MORNING

8:30-9:00   Registration and preconference balloting on the question

Assembly (Room 100)

Call to Order—by the Director of the Conference

Welcome to the Conference—by the Principal of the University High School

Welcome to the University School—by the President of the Student Council of the University High School

9:15   Demonstration panel discussion on the question by four university students, led by the Head Moderator of the Conference

9:45   Explanation of procedures to be followed—by the Head Moderator

10:00   ROUND TABLE I—Would a world federal government including all of the present members of the UN be preferable to the UN?

A. Would it promote peace more effectively?

B. Would it promote international cooperation more effectively?

C. Would its advantages compensate for the sacrifice of national sovereignty involved?

11:00 ASSEMBLY—Panel discussion to synthesize the conclusions reached in the round-table sessions, led by the Head Moderator

11:50 LUNCH

FRIDAY AFTERNOON

1:30 ROUND TABLE II—Would a world federal government without the Russian bloc of states be preferable to the UN?

A. Would it preserve peace more effectively?

B. Would it promote international cooperation more effectively?

2:30 ASSEMBLY—Panel discussion to synthesize reports of the round tables

3:15 ROUND TABLE III—Could world federal government be instituted by amending the Charter of the UN?

A. Could amendments, if adopted, transform the UN into a world federal government?

B. Would any one of the Big Five oppose the necessary amendments?

C. Could the opposition of one of the Big Five block the amending process?

4:15 ASSEMBLY—Panel discussion to synthesize the reports of the round tables

5:00 Adjournment until 8:30 A.M., Saturday Morning

FRIDAY EVENING

8:30 Program of one-act plays by the University School Players

SATURDAY MORNING

8:30 ROUND TABLE IV—Could world federal government be instituted now by developing "regional arrangements" within the framework of the UN Charter?

A. Would regional arrangements accomplish the purposes of world federal government?

B. Could such regional arrangements be achieved now?

9:30 ASSEMBLY—Panel discussion to synthesize reports of the round tables

10:00 ROUND TABLE V—How would an attempt to institute world federal government now affect international relations?

A. Would it weaken or strengthen the UN?

B. Would it make World War III more or less probable?

11:00 ASSEMBLY—Panel discussion to synthesize reports of the round tables

Report of Evaluation Committee

Announcements

Summary of conclusions reached by the Conference— by the Head Moderator

Distribution of post-conference ballots on world government

12:00 Adjournment

The summary of conclusions read at the closing assembly was as follows:

A majority of the conference are of the opinion that a world federal government including all members of the United Nations would be more effective than the United Nations both in preserving peace and in promoting international cooperation, and that the advantages of such an organization would compensate for the surrender of national sovereignty involved. Some members of the conference feel, however, that without the Slavic nations a world government would aggravate the tension between East and West and increase the likelihood of war. Those who favor proceeding without Russia do so largely in the expectation, not shared by some others, that Russia and her satellites eventually would join the new organization.

The conference is almost unanimously agreed that world government could not be instituted now by amending the Charter of the United Nations. While the United Nations could be transformed into a world government by amending the present Charter if the amendments were unopposed, Russia would almost certainly block the processes by refusing to ratify the amendments. The conference is also agreed that while it would be feasible to develop regional arrangements within the framework of the United Nations, the result would not be world government as this conference understands it.

The conference is sharply divided over the wisdom of agitating now for world federal government. Some feel that agitation at this time would hasten the day on which world government could be instituted; others fear it would aggravate present international tensions and perhaps postpone the day on which such an organization could be set up.

In summary, the conference is generally favorable to the idea of world federal government if and when all nations can be persuaded to join it but does not think it feasible to institute such a government at this time.

It is interesting to note that a comparison of the ballots marked before and after the conference indicated some shift of opinion on the part of a large majority of the conferees. This was especially noticeable in the case of those who previously had been undecided; discussion helped most of them to get off the fence. The predominant shift of opinion was against pressing now for world federal government.

Two weeks after the close of the conference each participating school received a final communication including statistics on attendance, a statement of the result of the shift-of-opinion ballot, a copy of the summary of conclusions reached, a copy of the report of the evaluation committee, and an announcement of the appointment of a conference committee for the following year.

According to the reports of students who attended and of teachers who accompanied them, the conference was a significant educational experience. Probably in no other way could conferees have gained so much in intellectual stimulation, clarification of thought, and practical knowledge of the democratic process. For young people—as well as for their elders—the educational value of a discussion conference is beyond question.

Its practical value in the conduct of affairs in many areas of public life has also been repeatedly demonstrated. The discussion conference is rapidly becoming one of our important democratic institutions.

References

Chapin, Leland T., "The Discussion Techniques of the Brookings Institution," *The Quarterly Journal of Speech,* December, 1948, p. 459.

Dunn, Frederick S., *The Practice and Procedure of International Conferences,* Baltimore: Johns Hopkins Press, 1929.

Gulley, Halbert E., *Discussion, Conference, and Group Process,* New York: Holt, Rinehart and Winston, Inc., 1960, Chap. 16.

Pastuhov, Vladimir D., *A Guide to the Practice of International Conferences,* New York: Columbia University Press, 1945.

Poole, D. C., "The Conference Method: As Taught at the School of Public and International Affairs at Princeton," *Educational Record,* 17 (August, 1936), p. 169.

APPENDIX

A. Case Problems for Practice in Discussion

THE CASE PROBLEM. To develop judgment and skill in the application of theory the student must spend a good deal of time in discussion. For this reason frequent class periods are devoted to sessions for practice with the class divided into groups of about seven each. Most of the discussions are of the multiple-choice case problems listed in the pages of this appendix. Early in the term the groups discuss four of the short problems during one class period; later they discuss one long problem each period. The student is not to study in advance the problem, or problems, to be discussed.

For a full discussion of class use of multiple-choice case problems and procedures for evaluating student performance in practice discussion turn to Appendix B.

Short Multiple-Choice Problems, Each to Be Studied for Two Minutes and Discussed for Seven Minutes

1.[1] Louis, plant services foreman, seemed to be reluctant to have his men move the plant cafeteria because he hadn't been informed of the intended move decided upon at a high-level conference.

What course of action should management have followed in this situation?

[1] Problems 1-15 are taken or adapted with permission of the author from "A Study of the Attitudes of Industrial Management Personnel toward Communication," unpublished doctoral dissertation by Dr. Dwight L. Freshley, Ohio State University, 1955.

2. Kildar, the foreman, had to go out of the plant for a couple of hours and instructed Mathews, his assistant, to start the crew on a rush order the second hour. Mathews failed to issue the instruction, the rush order was started late, and Kildar was severely reprimanded. When he saw Mathews, he demanded, "whaddya trying to do, have me fired?"

How should Kildar have handled this situation?

3. The staff meeting was discussing the lack of employees' general knowledge of the Cooperville plant management and its problems.

In what way should management attempt to acquaint employees with the activities and problems of management?

4. Franklin, a floor manager, arrived at his store's shoe department to find many customers and no sale shoes on the tables. He had sent Helwig, the salesman in charge, a memo four days previously asking him to have the girls set up the display. Helwig's explanation was that he could not remember receiving the memo.

After the shoes have been put on display, what action should Franklin take?

5. The executive staff is meeting to decide when and where to release information about a proposed plan of reorganization that will affect employees and will be of considerable interest to other business firms and to the public. The president is under pressure from some business editors to provide them with news about it.

How should the information be released?

6. Thorndike, the plant manager, had begun weekly informal luncheon conferences to which he was inviting a foreman and three assistant foremen. Sewell, a young assistant foreman, twenty-four years old, was eager to attend. "Man, will I tell him what I think of this lousy inspection idea of his!" His boss, Wilson, restrained him: "Aren't you ever gonna learn that you just don't go around arguing with the plant manager?"

How should Sewell conduct himself at these conferences?

7. Hargrave, a personnel interviewer, had strong convictions on the many benefits of the art of listening. Armstrong, an execu-

tive vice president, claimed, "I'm more of a realist myself. When I can settle an argument by being a good listener, O.K., but I haven't got time to play chaplain any other time."

What course of action should management follow in this connection?

8. In the interest of safety and economy, management began clamping down in certain areas in the plant. Because towels and lounges were sometimes burned in the girls' washrooms, a memorandum was issued forbidding smoking in these rooms. This caused much resentment among women employees, and they registered a complaint to management, who ignored it. Several weeks later when invitations were sent out to employees requesting attendance at a company picnic, few employees even returned the reply card.

What policy should management follow in regard to the regulations under which employees work?

9. Carter, the supervisor, instructed the unloading crew at 3:00 P.M. that more lumber was coming in late and would have to be unloaded that day. Not realizing that the lumber was green, the crew didn't stack it properly and the work had to be done over.

What course of action should Carter have followed in instructing the unloading crew?

10. At a Monday morning staff meeting, the industrial relations assistant stated that the latest information booklet on the company's retirement income plan was meeting with much success. Wednesday, Upshaw, the industrial relations director, was having coffee with several of the employees and when the subject got around to retirement income, one of the men asked, "Yeah, Mr. Upshaw, how does this thing work?"

What should Mr. Upshaw do now?

11. Mr. Ackerman was a conscientious foreman and eager for advancement. He caused Garrison, the plant manager, no trouble and always turned in reports of satisfactory conditions in his department. Lately, however, rumors have reached Garrison that there is considerable unrest among certain workers in Ackerman's department.

In the future what should be Ackerman's policy in regard to reporting what goes on in his department?

12. In an executive training program the discussion got around to face-to-face communication. It was lauded as being a good method. Jergensen, a young executive, maintained it was ineffective in many cases, citing the example of an associate who went into the plant and tried to be friendly with the employees and got a cold response.

With what attitude should an executive approach face-to-face communication with his employees?

13. At the County Treasurer's office a coffee break was established recently by management. It was planned that several members from the division were to go out at the same time. This became a social period for the whole division. The office manager then posted a schedule of which members of the division were to leave at what time. He felt they were still getting as much time and that he was doing them a favor by relieving the congestion at the cafeteria. But considerable griping occurred.

What should the office manager do now?

14. While a new building was being constructed each of two sections of clerk-typists were jealously afraid that the improved facilities would go to the other. This climaxed a long rivalry between the sections. Some clerks also felt insecure about status within their own group.

What course of action should management follow in this situation?

15. The editor of the Sparks plant monthly publication and the industrial relations director were discussing what topic should get the biggest play in an important issue. The editor insisted that compliments on jobs well done always took top priority. The industrial relations director claimed the coming reorganization plan, which would open up new jobs and provide some promotions, was more important.

What tpe of material should get the biggest play in the important issue under discussion?

16.[2] Foreman J. approached one of his men and gave him what ordinarily would have been considered a routine order. The man turned and replied angrily, "You go to hell. I won't do it."

What opening remarks by the foreman would promise the best handling of this situation?

17. The Cadbury Company had been doing well financially, and the officers proposed to distribute annually $100,000 in 7 percent preferred stock to their 1,200 employees on the basis of length of service. Some might receive as much as two or three $100 shares; others would receive fractional shares. Thus, some might get as much as $21 in annual dividends, others less than $7. The purposes of the proposed distribution were to discourage turnover and, if possible, to discourage the intermittent strikes that had lately held up production.

What action should the Company take in connection with this proposal?

18. The personnel manager administered an intelligence test to all employees before hiring them. Miss L. made an impressively high score, but he was obliged to start her on a simple repetitive job, as no other job was open at the time. She made no complaint and did the work well. A week later he transferred her to a better job where she could use her mind and earn more money. At the end of the week she announced that she wished to quit and offered the following explanation: "I don't like this new job. On the old one I could marry a prince every day if I wanted to."

How should the personnel manager handle this situation?

19. The F. Corporation manufactures and packages chocolate-covered candies in a wide range of qualities and prices. On the afternoon before Christmas all employees were handed identical gayly wrapped packages, each apparently containing two pounds of the company's product. Few employees showed surprise or interest in receiving the packages, and many returned to their

[2] Problems 16-21 are taken or adapted from *A Human Relations Casebook for Executives and Supervisors,* by Frances S. Drake and Charles A. Drake. Copyright 1947, McGraw-Hill Book Company, Inc. Used by permission.

work without opening them. A few did open their packages, however, and then the trouble began. The boxes contained the lowest grade product made by the company. "The cheapskates!" one exclaimed. Several threw their packages into waste cans. A few, however, when the supervisor's back was turned, emptied their boxes and refilled them with high quality candy. This reaction has come to the attention of management.

What Christmas gift policy should the firm follow in the future?

20. When Miss T. was hired at the local factory, the test given her by the personnel manager indicated that she should soon become an unusually efficient operator. In the training period before going onto a piece-work basis, she was soon turning out twice as much work as the other new girls. She was then moved to a piece-work job but soon dropped her rate of production to the average level of the other girls on the job. "One of the girls told me not to kill myself," she said, "and the other girls got mad and wouldn't talk to me, so I just made up my mind I'd take it easy." Miss T. also realized that outproducing the other girls by a wide margin might very likely lower the piece rate for every one.

What should Miss T. have done in this situation?

21. J., the new employment manager, watching a baseball game among workers during a lunch period, noticed one player, a boy of twenty and a new employee, whose movement seemed extremely awkward and inaccurate. He noticed also that the boy had a speech defect. Later, in an interview with him, J. became suspicious that the boy was not mentally normal, and an intelligence test revealed that he was a high-grade moron. The record showed that on his present job he had had several minor accidents, though his production rate was fairly good.

What should J. do about this situation?

22.[3] Mary Smith, an unmarried girl, works under your super-

[3] Problems 22-24 are taken or adapted with permission of the publisher from William J. McLarney, *Management Training: Cases and Principles,* Homewood, Ill.: Richard D. Irwin, Inc., 1954.

vision on a repetitive job requiring intermittent attention in order to avoid the formation of scrap. She has been one of the best operators in your department, but recently a large portion of her work has been defective. The unsatisfactory work began at about the same time as the introduction into the department of a new unmarried male employee, in whom Mary has been showing considerable interest.

What should you do?

23. As head of a department in a small factory you supervise twenty employees. Production is behind in your department, and your men have been putting in a good deal of overtime. You receive a telephone call from the wife of one of your men, requesting that you not allow her husband to work overtime because he uses it as an excuse for not coming home until late at night. You have noticed that his production has been falling off lately.

What should you do?

24. One of your best and most faithful workers at the factory has been coming late almost every morning for a month. His wife is ill, and he has had to assume many of her responsibilities in caring for the two children of school age. He tries to make it on time every morning; in fact, he rushes so much that you are afraid he may have an accident. His tardiness has a bad effect on the other workers in your department.

As supervisor of the department what should you do in this situation?

25. It has been the policy of your company to allow employees to borrow small pieces of plant equipment for their personal use after hours. Carl, a janitor, has been borrowing a floor sander and polisher every week end for the past six months. You have just learned that he has been renting this equipment to other people for their use.

As supervisor of the plant janitorial staff what should you do?

26. The management of a factory was trying to increase efficiency and the production rate. An industrial psychologist was brought in. But the employees were not happy to have the psy-

chologist roaming about looking over their shoulders. It began to look as if the union might step in.

What should management do in this situation?

27. Mary F., who works at a sewing factory, ran a sewing-machine needle through her finger. As superintendent of the factory you sent her to the company doctor. He declared it was a clean wound and sent her back to work without giving her a tetanus shot as a precaution against lockjaw. The company is responsible for payment of all expenses incurred by a worker in connection with a job-connected injury.

What should you do?

28. A foreman is suspicious that one of his workers is connected with the Communist party and may eventually influence other workers. The suspected employee, however, is respected by and popular with his fellow workers and is competent and efficient at his job.

In this situation what, if anything, should the foreman do?

29. Mr. Smith and Mr. Jones both worked at the same plant and had been good friends for several years. Smith, being more aggressive, was promoted and is now Jones's boss. Smith is getting along very well with all of his men except Jones, who has been causing a lot of trouble because he is jealous of Smith.

What should Smith do about the situation?

30. Your job is production foreman in an automotive-parts fabricating plant. Company policy regarding giving credit for suggestions made by employees is to reward the first person who turns in a useful suggestion in written form. John has developed an idea concerning a manufacturing problem. He is ready to write it up and turn it in, but George, a second employee, learns of the idea and beats John by turning it in first in written form. These facts are known to you as the foreman. As the idea is a very useful one, you should reward one of the employees.

What should you do?

31. Almost from the beginning of the term you have suspected that your instructor in the course on political systems was giving

his lectures a pro-Communist slant. Once he invited you and several other students in the course to spend an evening with him in his home. Most of the conversation was about politics and by the end of the evening you felt convinced that the instructor, whether avowedly a Communist or not, was following the Communist party line. He suggested that the same group come to his home again the next week to continue the discussion.

What should you do?

32. Mary K. is a senior in her last quarter at a large university. Her home is three hundred miles from the university; while at school she lives in her sorority house several blocks from the campus. During the past summer she became engaged to a young man at home. The wedding date is set for the week end of graduation. One of her final term courses is a required five-hour course with Professor G. On three separate occasions she has explained to the professor that she is taking a long week end to go home and work on wedding plans, each time missing classes on the preceding Friday and the following Monday. In addition she recently was out of school three days with a bad cold, as evidenced by a note from her housemother. Her test grades have been below average, and she has missed certain performance assignments in the course which are virtually impossible to make up. She realizes that she is in danger of failing in the course. It is now three weeks till the end of the term and she finds that another long week end at home has become necessary.

What action should the professor take?

33. George C. Activity, a college junior, has many responsibilities around the campus. He is an honor student, also. During the term he has been absent fifteen times from Philosophy 792, a five-hour seminar course in which participation in class discussion is an important part of course work. The policy of the Department of Philosophy on absences is that only those noted in the official bulletin published in the campus newspaper as "excused" will be regarded as excused by the Department. Five of George's absences were "excused" through an announcement in the campus newspaper. He has had a bad cold almost con-

stantly but he has not consulted a physician about it. On numerous occasions he has gone home to comfort an ailing mother. He has usually told the professor his reason for absence and has handed in all written work and made up all tests.

To what extent should the professor permit these absences to alter George's grade in the course?

34. You, a senior, have noticed that a sophomore whom you know well and who works near you in the physics laboratory often slips small pieces of equipment into his pocket and carries them away from the laboratory. You have never seen him return any of them. Some of the pieces are of considerable value and you suspect that he is either selling them or using them to equip a small laboratory of his own.

What should you do?

35. A few days before the final examination you learn by chance that another student in one of your courses is in possession of a copy of the examination questions to be used in the final examination and that he is passing it around among his friends in the course. You know that several students in the course have already seen it and you suspect that nearly a third of those in the course have seen it.

What should you do?

36. Jack S., an unmarried student at a large state university, is scheduled to graduate at the end of the current term. His four years at the university have been financially difficult, and Jack has been forced to work at outside jobs the entire time, though his scholastic record is excellent in spite of this. He has lived at a very inexpensive rooming house some distance from the campus during the past term. The house is not registered with the university but has never been involved with the school in a complaint. Three weeks before graduation Jack's landlord called the office of the dean of men and complained that Jack had not paid his rent for the preceding month or the present month in spite of reasonable efforts to collect the rent.

How should the university react to the landlord's complaint?

37. A regulation of the university requires that graduation fees be paid four weeks in advance of the graduation date; otherwise a diploma will be denied. Three weeks before graduation John T. was called to the registrar's office and informed that he would not graduate because his fees had been received five days after the deadline. John complained that the fault was not his, since the final notification of fees due had not reached him until after the final day had passed. When it was pointed out that the final notice had been mailed three weeks in advance of the final date, John replied that his was sent to the wrong address. He had moved since the term started and the notice had not been forwarded promptly.

What action should the registrar take?

38. Professor Anthrax of the Biology Department followed the policy in his Biology 401, an introductory course, of making the following assignments: thirty pages of reading in the textbook for each of the three lecture periods per week, one hundred pages of outside reading per week with notes taken for periodic inspection by the professor, and a term paper to be handed in at the end of the course.

What action should students in the course take regarding these assignments?

39. Elinore, a college junior, is enrolled in Speech 402. She needs a B in the course to "go active" in her sorority. If she does not improve her scholastic average to the required level this term, she will be dropped by the sorority. In a private conference she has told the instructor in the course of her need to get at least a B in the course.

How should the instructor react to her request for a B?

40. Jim is a very smart student in Commerce College but is of the opinion that if a student can get the necessary knowledge without attending class, it isn't necessary for him to attend. However, the instructor has made it clear that he thinks a student should not miss more than ten classes a term. During the first three weeks of school Jim missed eight classes; during the

fourth week he missed three more. He made an A on the mid-term examination.

What should the instructor do about these absences?

41. John is the star halfback on the C.U. football team. He is the most important member of the team, so far this year making 75 percent of the touchdowns. But John is a night owl who has no regard for training rules. He drinks, smokes, and carouses until all hours of the night. The coach and the other members of the team know of this.

What should the coach do?

42. Jane, a member of X Sorority, studied very hard for her history mid-term exam. When she was taking the exam, she noticed that one of her sorority sisters was cheating. Jane has not been too friendly with this girl. Jane knew the exam would be graded "on the curve."

What should Jane do in this situation?

43. James has turned in a final paper to his history professor which is far better than anything he has done before. The professor suspects plagiarism, though after a careful investigation he cannot prove it.

What should the professor do?

44. According to the housing rules of a certain university, male students are permitted to live in private apartments provided they are twenty-one years old or have been in the armed service. Female students must live in university-approved rooming houses or in dormitories. The female students feel that they also should be permitted to live in private apartments after they have reached the age of twenty-one. They have petitioned the university for permission to do so.

How should the university react to this petition?

45. Eight students at X University have known for some time that for $5 they could buy a copy of a stolen exam that is soon to be used in a course they all take. The eight contributed to a fund of $5, and one of them, John, who had a car, drove to another town and purchased the exam. All eight studied it.

These facts, including the names of John and the other seven students, have become known to the professor a day before the exam is to be given.

What should the professor do?

46. Betty was a twenty-two-year-old college junior. While vacationing in Florida between terms, she met a dental student— a senior who had one more year to complete his training. Arriving back on the campus, she began dating him about twice a week. She heard often from his friends of his plan for future marriage with her, though he never indicated this to her in any way. Betty was fond of him, enjoyed dating with him, and would have liked to continue the relationship. But she was not thinking of marriage in the immediate future and feared she might hurt the boy's feelings if the dating continued.

What should she do?

47. Julia O'Connor, a rather devout Catholic student at X University, was much attracted to Patrick Kelley, one of her classmates, and he seemed interested in her. When he asked her for a date, she accepted; several other dates followed. In the course of one of them, Pat made a chance remark clearly indicating that he was a Protestant, though he didn't seem to be an especially religious person. When he asked her for a fifth date, Julia was uncertain what to do.

What should Julia do?

48. A well-liked fifteen-year-old boy from a broker's home is caught stealing from a cash register in a small grocery store where he works. The owner has known the boy for a long time and has always thought highly of him. The sum stolen was about $25.

What should the owner do?

49. Miss Stevens, a sixth-grade teacher, was called into the office by the principal to fill out and sign a form he had prepared, in which the teacher was required to swear that she would never join a teachers' union which advocated use of a strike, that she would never raise her voice in talking to her "beloved

pupils," etc. Miss Stevens discovered that the other teachers also were being called in to sign this document.

What should Miss Stevens do?

50. You were driving your car alone at 4:00 A.M. on a lightly traveled mountain road when you struck and *apparently* killed a truck driver who had alighted from his truck and was crossing the road.

What should you do?

51. John Doe High School is installing facilities in classrooms for the use of instructional television. May Smith teaches American government. She fears that use of television will eventually deprive her of her job; so she refuses to use the facilities.

How should the school react to this situation?

52. Bill and Joan have been married for six months. During this time Joan's parents have continued to buy Joan clothes and other things she and Bill cannot afford to buy, as Bill's income is still a very modest one. Bill is beginning to resent this.

How should Bill handle this situation?

Long Multiple-Choice Problems, Each to Be Studied Ten Minutes and Discussed for Thirty Minutes

53. John and Mary are fairly typical college students from upper middle-class American homes. John is twenty years old and in his junior year in engineering; Mary is nineteen and a sophomore in home economics. They met a year and a half ago at school and have been dating steadily since that time. There is no question that they are really in love. Three months ago, with the consent of the four parents, they became engaged, and they wish to be married within the next three months.

Neither John nor Mary is self-supporting. Their tuition and most of their expenses are paid by their parents, who in both cases are fairly well-to-do. It will take John two more full years, including summers, to complete his engineering degree, if he is not drafted into the army before then. His draft board is following a tough policy and may not defer him, although he is in the upper half of his class. Mary can complete her degree in about two years and should have no difficulty in getting a teaching position after graduation.

The parents, though not entirely happy about the marriage plans, have promised to continue giving them, while they are in school, the same financial support they are now receiving.

What should this couple do about marriage plans?

54. Norman L., a university student, is Jewish, although neither his name nor his appearance suggests it. He is aware of the antisemitism in the country and feels that being a Jew is a handicap with which he does not wish to burden himself. Accordingly, he has not made his Jewish origin known on the campus. He has not found it difficult to follow this policy, as he is in any case not at all religious in the conventional sense. Most of his friends, male and female, are non-Jews. On the whole he gets along very well with them.

Recently, while he was in conversation with several friends, one member of the group made some patently antisemitic remarks. Norman bristled inwardly but at the moment was undecided as to how he should respond. He felt guilty at letting the remarks go unanswered; any good citizen, he thought, whether Jewish or not, should challenge such remarks. Yet, he feared that he could not challenge them effectively without betraying his identity as a Jew. Besides, he said to himself, if he challenged them and revealed his identity, he might be accused of an unreasonable bias in favor of the Jewish religion.

What should Norman have done?

55. In the College of Dentistry at X University the honor system is employed in all examinations. During examinations no proctor is ever in the room. Under the system all students are pledged to observe the following rules in connection with examinations:

1. No cheating of any kind is permitted.

2. Any student observing another cheating is morally obligated to report the student cheating to the college authorities.

3. If a student observes another cheating and does not report it, he is liable to the same penalty as the cheater. In this connection all students are under moral obligation, not only to report any cheating observed, but also to report the failure of a student to report cheating he has observed.

John and Tom are first-year students in the college and are good friends. Both are average students, both are pledged to the same dental fraternity, and both are very popular with their classmates as evidenced by the fact that both have been nominated for the presidency of their freshman class.

During a final examination John saw Tom cheat by reading from the paper of the student seated next to him. Elliot also saw Tom cheat. John saw that Elliot saw the cheating. John also saw that Elliot saw that John saw the cheating.

What should John do?

56. Professor Dearborn is a teacher at a large state university which does not use the honor system. Examinations are closely proctored, and other precautions are taken to prevent cheating. But Professor Dearborn believes in individual integrity. He does not enforce the proctoring regulation, especially when he has a reasonable opportunity to avoid it. He had such an opportunity when a student missed the final examination and had to make it up. Professor Dearborn gave the student several essay questions, provided him with a chair and table in his office, and left for the library after telling him to leave his examination paper on the desk when he had finished.

The professor returned in about an hour and a half to find the student gone and the examination paper on his desk. On reading the paper he found that it had obviously been cribbed from several books he had left in his office; of this there could be no doubt.

The professor had authority to give the student an *E* on the paper, to give him an *E* in the course, or even to report him to the dean for disciplinary action. "However," he reflected, "I knew that this student was standing only a *D* in the course when I left him alone in my office. Did I not put temptation in his path? Am I, rather than the student, mainly responsible for his dishonesty?"

What should Professor Dearborn do about this incident?

57.[4] Mr. Franklin, supervisor of the plant electrical shop, decided that an electrical conduit would have to be run from one section of the plant to another distant section. To avoid laying it under the floor, laying it along the wall, or suspending it from the ceiling, he planned to run it through the ventilating system. The ventilating system consisted of square metal pipes large enough for a man to crawl through and drag the conduit after him. The job would be disagreeable, but in Mr. Franklin's opinion, not dangerous. He asked Walker, one of the electricians, to do the job. Walker refused, and the following conversation took place:

FRANKLIN: Why won't you do it?

WALKER: It's too dangerous.

FRANKLIN: Where's any danger involved?

WALKER: It gets mighty hot in those ventilators. A guy could pass out in there and you'd never get him out. And another thing—it's easy for you white-collar fellows to sit in your cool offices and dream up these jobs. I don't see you doing anything to get your clothes messed up.

FRANKLIN: Walker, I do my job as I'm told and I expect you to do the same. But since you have made that last statement, I'll tell you what we'll do. You and I are going through that ventilator with the conduit, and I'm going to lead the way. If you refuse to follow me, you are through with this company. If you do follow me, you will be suspended from work for three days for forcing me to get the job done this way.

Walker followed him through the ventilator and was suspended for three days.

[4] This problem is adapted with permission of the publisher from Cruickshank, Henry and Keith Davis, *Cases in Management,* Homewood, Ill.: Richard D. Irwin, Inc., 1954.

How should Franklin have handled this situation at the time when Walker refused to obey the order?

58.[5] Mr. Welty, publisher of a newspaper, in 1951 employed a total staff of about two hundred. He prided himself on the high morale among his employees and on their loyalty to him and to the paper. "You may call my kind of management paternalism," he once said, "but I know all of my employees personally and don't have to buy their friendship and loyalty." Though unaware that he had any personnel problem, Mr. Welty had a personnel consultant make a survey and evaluation of the organization. The survey indicated a high level of morale among employees except in the pressroom.

To his astonishment Mr. Welty learned that in the pressroom morale and production were very low, that nearly all of the thirty-eight men employed in that department were bitter in their feeling against the foreman, Harry Fitzpatrick. They considered him arbitrary, vindictive, and indifferent to their welfare. As evidence of his indifference they pointed to the deplorable condition of the locker room. Six of the apprentices, former servicemen, were especially sour on Fitzpatrick. He was down on all ex-servicemen, they said, and constantly abused and insulted them.

Shocked by these disclosures, Mr. Welty toured the pressroom and locker room, putting questions to some of the workmen. He then ordered the locker room repaired and cleaned up and after a long talk with Fitzpatrick reprimanded him sharply. After twenty-three years with the firm and thirteen years as foreman, he insisted, Fitzpatrick should know how to treat employees better.

A few months later, on again checking the situation in the pressroom, Mr. Welty found no improvement in employee morale and no improvement in Fitzpatrick's relations with his workmen. To Mr. Welty it seemed obvious that something more

[5] Problems 58-64 are taken or adapted from Robert Dubin, *Human Relations in Administration: The Sociology of Organization* © 1951 by Prentice-Hall, Inc., Englewood Cliffs, N. J. Reprinted by permission.

drastic than a verbal reprimand was necessary. Reluctant to dismiss Fitzpatrick, he appointed an acting foreman for the pressroom and for a one-year period assigned Fitzpatrick to supervise the installation of new presses in another part of the plant. "This may be a cowardly decision," he admitted to himself, "but a lot can happen in a year and I'll cross this bridge when I come to it a year from now."

How should Mr. Welty have handled this situation after his second visit to the pressroom?

59. William Dixon, a recent liberal-arts graduate, had no specific training for work in advertising but thought he had background and skill that would be useful in that work when he had acquired the specific knowledge needed. Mr. Strauss, head of the advertising department of the Raymond Optical Company, agreed with him and was glad to see him employed to work under his supervision. Dixon, recently married, was anxious to make good on the job as a start on a career.

He began by doing odd jobs in the office, but soon Mr. Strauss was assigning him the simpler jobs in copy writing, writing short pieces for the monthly magazine sent out to all of the company's customers, and writing institutional ads for trade journals. Meanwhile, in his spare time he read all of the ads used by the company during the past dozen years and even did some library work to gain more knowledge of optics and the history of the optical field. Dixon undertook all of the jobs assigned to him with enthusiasm and worked hard at them. He felt he was doing a pretty good job and that Mr. Strauss thought so too, though Strauss had said nothing definitely in commendation of his work. About the office, however, it was noticed that while he had pleasant relations with everyone, Dixon lacked intimate friends among the office staff.

That Christmas, the annual convention of the company salesmen was planned as an especially gala affair. Strauss was in charge of the convention and with his staff worked many evenings and week ends to make the necessary arrangements. Dixon assisted in this work, setting up displays, etc., working until well past midnight on the two days before the convention. Mr. Strauss complimented him on the job he was doing.

The convention lasted three days. Dixon was down at the hotel early each day and stayed through the day at the exhibits, meeting the salesmen and explaining the exhibits. He was included in the general invitation to take part in the dinner meetings and the fun that followed them. However, he preferred to go home when the exhibits closed in the late afternoon, and took no part in any of the evening social affairs.

Two weeks after the convention Strauss called Dixon into his office and fired him, giving him two weeks' pay in lieu of notice. It was painful for Strauss to tell Dixon that he was through. He pointed out that he had been satisfied with Dixon's work in the office but that he did not think he had the proper attitude to make a good advertising man. He told Dixon that he did not seem to mix well with people and that it was a distinct disappointment that he had seemed to avoid really participating in the convention. He pointed out that the company was small and depended on close personal relationships to grease the way for effective cooperation in the company. He said he was sorry Dixon did not fit into the picture and wished him luck in finding a new job.

Assuming that the ability to meet people easily, and genuinely to enjoy their company, was a prime condition of success in Dixon's job, how should Strauss have handled Dixon from the first interview up to the time when he decided to fire him?

60. Miss Winkler has been employed by the River Manufacturing Company under the supervision of Mr. Wilson, as the bookkeeper in charge of accounts receivable. Her work has been exceptionally good, and Mr. Wilson often has commended the accuracy, neatness, and currency of her records.

Mr. Watson, a certified public accountant and field representative of the accounting firm of Smith and Company, was auditing the River Manufacturing Company's books. When he came to accounts receivable, he wished to examine the ledger cards and to run an adding machine tape on them for the purpose of checking the total against the control ledger. After engaging Miss Winkler pleasantly in conversation, he asked if he might see her ledger cards. "What do you want them for?" she asked sharply. He explained that he would need to run a tape on them in connection with his audit of the books. Miss Winkler took a tape from her desk and handed it to him with these words: "I have already run the figures on this tape; and you can use it. It will save you a lot of time and bother." Her manner made it clear that she expected him to be appreciative of her having gone so far beyond the call of duty to help him.

Mr. Watson thanked her, but added that it was his practice to run a tape himself, and added: "It will be nice to be able to use your figures to check my own accuracy. May I have the cards now?" Her reply was an explosive "No!" And she immediately stormed into the office of her supervisor, Mr. Wilson.

"That man doesn't think I do my work accurately," she said. "He refused to use my figures. I did all that work to help him and then he turns up his nose at it." After listening to her patiently, Mr. Wilson said: "Well, everyone knows how snoopy these auditors are. And after all, if they do not want to accept such generous favors as you thoughtfully provided for them, it is their business. Not everyone appreciates human kindness and consideration and maybe auditors are in that class."

Miss Winkler returned to her desk and with icy politeness handed Mr. Watson the ledger cards.

How should Mr. Wilson have handled this situation when Miss Winkler stormed into his office?

61. For thirty-seven years Frederick Schmidt was the principal owner and the dominant figure in the management of the Modern Manufacturing Company, which for three generations had been a family business. He prided himself on knowing all of his several hundred employees by name and on taking a warm personal interest in their welfare. "Every employer is his brother's keeper," he once said, "and such factories as ours realize this fact."

The record indicates that Mr. Schmidt's interest in his employees was genuine and that for a lifetime it had dominated his relations with them. As early as 1897 an Employee's Aid Society was established. In 1910 a Foremen's Club was set up, and in the following year a technical library was provided for employees who wished to improve themselves. From the beginning of the Schmidt regime liberal awards were made for length of service, and in 1912 employees who had been with the firm for thirty years were given a two-month vacation with pay, given a bonus of $1,000, and provided with travel money which enabled some of them who had been born abroad to visit their birthplaces. An elaborate company picnic was held each summer, and the annual Christmas party was accompanied by the liberal distribution of bonuses and food baskets. As early as 1919 the 48-hour week with time and a half for overtime was standard. A bank account was set up by the firm for each child born to an employee, and the parents were provided for one year with the use of a baby's crib without cost. When a child graduated from high school, he received a cash gift. Other activities and facilities provided free by the firm included a band, a playground, an athletic association, a park and clubhouse, a gymnasium, and a skating rink. As the years of his service drew near to an end, Frederick Schmidt looked back on a lifetime of service to the firm and its employees with pride and satisfaction.

During World War II, for the first time, a union attempted to organize the plant and began to distribute handbills at the factory gate. The management was frankly amused. What could the union offer their employees that they didn't have already? But the union won the election by an overwhelming majority.

Soon after, Mr. Schmidt retired, a bitter and broken man. He died the following year, his death hastened, some felt, by the shock.

What policy should Mr. Schmidt have followed through the years in his relations with his employees?

62. During World War II a steel plant was engaged in work of crucial importance to the war effort. In one department, responsible for an essential process in manufacturing the product,

seventy-five women were employed as tin turners. They were middle-aged women. Most of them had men folk in the war and were zealously patriotic and bitterly resentful of anyone they considered a "slacker." All employees were required by the firm's government contract to be members of the Metal Workers Union.

Among the women were two members of the religious sect known as Witnesses. Sect members are pacifists, and while the two women had no objection to working in the plant, they refused on religious grounds to attend patriotic meetings, to subscribe to war bonds, to stand at attention and salute the flag during public patriotic observances, etc. They were excellent workers with high seniority in their jobs and were loyal and active members of the union.

The other women gave the two offending workers the "silent" treatment, which the two took without complaining. Finally, the other women staged a wildcat strike and insisted they would not return to work as long as the two "slackers" were on the job with them.

Among additional facts in the situation were the following: The union was under pledge not to strike while the war was in progress. The union constitution contained a clause forbidding the union to discriminate against a worker because of his religion. The management was under obligation to the government to meet a production quota. Under its contract with the union the management could not dismiss a worker without cause, especially if the worker had seniority.

What should have been done in this situation?

63. For many years Mr. Peter Vallee, Vice President of the Savage Corporation, has combined the jobs of vice president in charge of production and labor-relations manager, in both of which he has been eminently successful. The firm's excellent record of good relations with the union has been due in part to the fact that Mr. Vallee knows in intimate detail every phase of production. He is the kind of executive who works with his sleeves rolled up and spends much of his time in the plant.

In rate discussions with union representatives, he has been completely master of the situation because he knows thoroughly the jobs on which rates are in dispute. And he has never been a man to discuss a problem in the abstract. When a dispute arises with the union he usually reaches for his hat and says, "Let's go out and look at the job." This practical competence and his reputation for integrity, straightforwardness, and fairness has built up a fine relation between union and management.

But at sixty-four he has found himself unable physically to handle both production and labor relations any longer, and labor relations have been turned over to Joseph Scoville. Scoville has not come up through the ranks, as did Vallee. In fact, his previous experience was with another firm. While in that firm, his work had nothing to do with labor relations, but he did observe how disputes were handled. There had been prolonged wrangles and tough battles even over trivial issues; negotiations between labor and management were rather formal and marked by a good deal of hostility on both sides. It was from this observation that Scoville had formed his ideas of labor relations.

His first problem on the new job involves a dispute on the loading dock. The company contends that the loading crew has been working at only about 70 percent efficiency, while the union insists that there are differences now in the loading work due to differences in design of the models being loaded into freight cars. After one fruitless session Scoville prepared for the next by getting figures on comparable operations at the plants of competitors, which showed that the loading operations in his own plant are below that of competitors in efficiency. When asked by the union for the source of his figures, he refused to give it, saying that the information was given to him in confidence. This provoked a tirade from the union representative, who accused him of underhanded methods and charged him with destroying good labor relations at the plant. After a stormy two hours, the session has adjourned without result.

How should Vallee handle this situation? Beginning at the time when he realized that he could no longer handle both jobs, what should he have done?

64. Jack Murphy, a good worker who had been employed for ten years in the foundry of the Miller Company, had his foot badly injured in an accident on the job. After he was able to hobble about, but a month before he was able to go back to the foundry, he told the personnel manager that he couldn't live on his payments from the state Workmen's Compensation fund and asked if he could be assigned temporarily to light work outside of the foundry, even if it had to be at a lower rate of pay. This meant, of course, that he would no longer receive payments from the compensation fund. The personnel manager found a job for him in the shipping department, but in view of his good record agreed to pay him at his regular rate as a foundry worker until he was able to go back to his old job. Jack was very grateful for this consideration.

But Jack's fellow workers in the foundry went on the war path. The company had no right, they said, to pay him a foundry-man's wages while he was working in the shipping department. In fact, it had no right to give him the temporary job at all; this was rank favoritism. When Hank was hurt a few months ago, he was not given a temporary job. "But he didn't ask for it," the personnel manager replied. "If he had, we probably could have found something for him." But the workmen were not satisfied with this answer. It was just such favoritism as this, they said, that had led them ten years ago to organize a union local at the plant.

What should have been management's policy in cases of this kind?

Single-Issue Problems, Each to Be Studied Ten Minutes and Discussed for Thirty Minutes

65.[6] The Maybrook and Campbell Hall road in Orange County runs approximately east and west. The Neelytown road enters it from the north. At the junction, the Neelytown road spreads out, turning by one fork toward the west in the direction of

[6] Problems 65-68 in this series are taken or adapted with permission of the publisher from Frank C. McKinney and Mary Eula McKinney, *A Case Book in Discussion*, The Ronald Press Company, New York.

Campbell Hall and by the other fork to the east, or in the direction of Maybrook. Between the forks of the road at the junction is a triangular grass plot. While the Neelytown road at this point joins the other road, it does not cross it. Persons coming down the Neelytown road must turn either to the right or to the left to enter the Maybrook–Campbell Hall road.

At nine o'clock in the morning, on an August day, Anzie W. Shuman, a conductor on the Lehigh & Hudson Railroad, was driving his car in a westerly direction along the Maybrook road approaching the Neelytown road. He had other railroad employees in the car with him and was going to his home in Campbell Hall. As he approached the junction of these two roads, he blew his horn several times and slowed down to about eighteen miles an hour. In the direction he was driving, the Neelytown road entered at his right, or from the north. His view was obstructed. So also was the view of any person coming down the Neelytown road. Trees and bushes in full foliage obscured the view of all approaching vehicles until the actual intersection of the highways was reached.

Chauncey Hall and his wife, Anna Hall, on the way to Maybrook, were coming along the Neelytown road in their Dodge car. Their view of Shuman in his Ford car was obstructed by the same trees, bushes, and tall grass which obstructed Shuman's view of them. The two cars collided at the intersection. Shuman was killed.

Question: Was Hall responsible for causing the death of Shuman?

66. Around the turn of the century a lecturer or writer might secure the protection of a copyright for a literary effort, provided he had not already "dedicated to the public," or given to the public generally, either his lecture or its publication.

Nicols, prominent at that time as an author and lecturer upon various scientific subjects, delivered from memory, though it was in uncopyrighted manuscript form, a lecture at the Workingmen's College upon "The Dog as the Friend of Man." The audience was admitted to the room by tickets issued gratuitously by a committee representing the college. Pitman, the author of a system of shorthand writing, attended the lecture and took notes, nearly verbatim, in shorthand and afterward published the lecture in shorthand in his magazine. The magazine, written entirely in shorthand, was published commercially for use by students of stenography. It consisted in part of stenographic reports of public speeches, with credit given to the speaker. Nicols sued Pitman to recover damages for the publication of his lecture.

Question: Should Nicols have won the suit?

67. One of the early rules of Berea College prohibited students from "entering eating houses and places of amusement in Berea not controlled by the college." The penalty for disobedience of the rule was dismissal from college.

One of the restaurants in the town was owned by a man named Graham. He claimed that the enforcement of the rule by the college would seriously injure his business. Accordingly, he sued the college to restrain it from enforcing the rule. He stated that the college had no right to take away the privileges of citizens, especially when the rules, if enforced, would injure the business of the town.

Evidence turned up to show that Graham had been a bootlegger and that he had previously been convicted as such.

Question: Should Graham have won the suit?

68. Purdue University in Indiana is supported, in part at least, by the state. The trustees of the university adopted a rule that no student would be permitted to join a Greek-letter or other secret society. The penalty was dismissal from college.

Hawley, a student who was not a member of a secret society, left the university in April, not expecting to return. Thereafter he joined a Greek-letter fraternity and later sought to return to Purdue. Before admitting him again to the university, the president demanded that he sign a pledge to the effect that when he left the university in April he was not a member of a secret society and that he would disconnect himself from the fraternity which he had joined in the meantime. Hawley refused to sign and brought an action in the courts to compel the university to accept him without requiring him to resign from the fraternity which he had joined after departing from Purdue. Question: Should Hawley have won the suit?

69.[7] The Case Drug Company in 1952 operated fourteen drugstores in a city of 50,000 population. In each store there was a prescription shop equipped with a stock of crude drugs and chemicals amounting in value to approximately $8,000. To dispense prescriptions, two registered pharmacists were needed in each store. They received an average salary of $4,000 a year. The average waste and spoilage amounted to $700 a store per year.

It was proposed that the firm open a separate prescription shop in the business district in which nothing but prescriptions would be sold. The plan was to take the prescription shop out of each of the fourteen stores and localize them in this central shop. By means of errand boys and telephones all of the stores would be within five minutes' time of the central shop. By centralizing, only one pharmacist would be needed in each store and nine in the main shop. This would mean a saving amounting to the salaries of five pharmacists. The plan would also mean that the central shop would eliminate loss from waste and spoilage, as stock would have a complete turnover approximately every two months. There also would be considerable reduction in the investment in drugs, since stock for the central shop would total only about $12,000.

On the other hand, it might be argued that a prescription shop lends an atmosphere of prestige to each store and gives the customers confidence in it; that if the prescriptions were not filled in the individual store, the customers would trade elsewhere; that this new system would mean paying pharmacist wages to a pharmacist in each of the stores while actually he would be little more than an ordinary clerk; that it might be doubtful whether five-minute service could be maintained between the central shop and its fourteen stores. In connection with cost of operation, it should be remembered that the central

[7] Problems 69 and 70 are taken or adapted with permission of the authors from Leland S. Winch, Harvey Cromwell, and Alan H. Monroe, *Interview Problems*, Cincinnati: Tri-State Offset Co., 1952.

store would be bringing in little if any income. It would serve principally as a service agency for the other stores. The fourteen stores would have to be remodeled to utilize the space previously occupied by prescription shops.

Question: Should a separate prescription shop have been opened?

70. The Century Cement Company makes a high grade of Portland cement and in 1952 maintained a daily production of 5,000 barrels. The limestone was brought in by rail and dumped into the storage pit, 200 yards from the mixing bin. The limestone had to be loaded into small cars by hand and pulled by a switch engine over a narrow-gauge track to the mixing bin. Here the cars dumped their loads, and the train of empty cars returned for reloading. The cycle was repeated four times a day in order to furnish enough limestone for the next day's grind.

The small dory engine used to pull the cars required steam in its boiler during the entire day, though it made only four trips of 400 yards each. Its efficiency was extremely low, and it cost about $20 per day to operate. One man was required to operate the engine, and four men were employed to load the cars. As these cars were handled roughly and exposed to the weather, depreciation and repairs were figured at 20 percent a year. The initial cost per car was $1,000, and ten cars made up the train.

The president of the company, Mr. Parker, had considered the installation of some type of continuous conveying system. Although he had no knowledge of engineering, he was anxious to have some method which would cost him less money than the train then in use. He called in a sales engineer, Mr. Anderson, a representative of the Chain Belt Company. Mr. Anderson recommended the installation of a belt conveyor, costing $50,000. Freight and installation would amount to $1,500, bringing the total cost to $51,500.

Only one man would be required to operate the system, and the maintenance would be only 4 percent of the initial cost per year. The power required to operate the conveyor would be a three-horsepower motor rather than the small dory engine used by the train.

Mr. Parker thought the system had merit, but disliked the expense. The company was operating at a profit under the old system. The four men who would no longer be needed had been with him for ten years, and Mr. Parker did not like to discharge them.

Question: Should the new system have been installed?

71. Bob R. is an engineering student who will graduate at the end of this year. He is twenty-eight years old and three years ago married a boyhood sweetheart. They now have a child of two and are expecting another. By working part time, Bob has been able to keep his family going. The struggle has been arduous both for him and his wife.

Looking ahead to his graduation, Bob has been investigating the job situation and finds it good. He has studied numerous opportunities and has narrowed the field down to two in which he is seriously interested. One job is at North American in Columbus, Ohio, the other at Consolidated Vultee in California. At North American, his job would be concerned with design of aircraft parts, a field in which he always has been interested. But he has heard from people already there, that the chief engineer of that division is a martinet and a very difficult person to work under. His salary at North American would be $8,000 a year, but since this plant is expanding rapidly, he feels sure he could get regular pay raises. At Consolidated, Bob would be doing jet research, an important field but not one in which he is specially interested. It is a field, however, in which newcomers can expect to rise rapidly. Bob would begin with a salary of $10,000 a year and work under a chief who is a leading expert in jet research but who shows little interest in his subordinates.

Since her family lives in Ohio, Bob's wife is not completely happy about moving to California. Yet, she has never been there and would like to see the state. Bob is indifferent about location but feels that his family deserves to have a trip and a change of scenery. Should he decide to move to California, Bob could borrow from his father $1,000 with which to make the move.

Question: Which job should Bob take?

B. Discussion of Multiple-Choice Case Problems

To insure that students do not study problems prior to assignment, the instructor does not indicate in advance which problems will be discussed on any particular day. As students study each problem preparatory to discussing it, the instructor writes on the blackboard or hands students copies of the five possible solutions of the problem from which a choice is to be made. While one of the five is known by the instructor to be the best in the opinion of subject-matter experts, he does not reveal at any time which is the preferred solution of any problem.

Class Routine

On a typical practice day, when four problems are to be discussed, the class routine is as follows: As students enter the room each is assigned to a group for the day, the composition of the groups being changed daily so that no group meets more than once. One member of the group may be designated as the moderator; he votes and participates in discussion as freely as the other members, but has a special responsibility for insuring that the discussion is orderly and productive. Another member, who does not vote or participate in the discussion, is designated as the clerk for the group. At the beginning of the hour he picks up from the instructor's desk a sufficient number of pre- and post-discussion ballots and a form on which at the end of the hour he will report to the instructor on the result of discussion in his group.

At a signal from the instructor the clerks distribute to each group member a copy of a prediscussion ballot. The student has two minutes in which to read the problem, which the instructor designates by number, and indicate on the signed ballot his prediscussion choice of best solution. The groups then discuss the problem for seven minutes, the instructor acting as timekeeper. At the end of that time, each student indicates on a signed ballot his postdiscussion choice of best solution. The clerk collects the ballots, and the instructor announces the second problem for the day. This procedure is continued through the class hour. At the close of the period the clerk reports to the instructor for each of the four problems each group member's pre- and postdiscussion choice of solution. Later in the term, when the groups are discussing one only of the longer problems during a class period, the routine is the same except that the groups have ten minutes to study and thirty minutes to discuss the problem.

Evaluation of Performance

When the class has discussed about twenty of the short problems, a class period is devoted to evalution of performance. At that time each student receives three grades, or class rankings, on his performance. The first is based on the proportion of times he chose the preferred solution before discussion, for he is learning in the course how to study a problem thoughtfully before discussing it. The second is based on the proportion of times he chose the preferred solution after discussion, for he is learning to listen open-mindedly and profit from discussion. The third is based on the percentage of members in his groups who chose the preferred solution after discussion, regardless of whether he agreed with them, for he is learning in the course to assume responsibility for the quality of the group product.

At the end of each practice day the instructor has transferred the data from the clerks' reports to permanent individual record sheets, one for each member of the class. The sheet is set up as indicated in the following, the sample looking as it might for the second period of evaluation.

SAMPLE STUDENT'S RECORD SHEET

NAME:

SHIFTS

R-W	Z	Ɉ Z
W-W	Z Z Z Z	Ɉ Z
W-R	Z Z Z Z	Z Z Z Z Z
R-ns	Ɉ Ɩ Ɩ Ɩ Ɉ Ɉ Ɉ Ɉ	Ɩ Ɩ Ɩ Z Z Ɩ Ɩ Z
W-ns	Ɩ Ɩ Ɩ	Ɩ Ɩ Ɩ
	(20)	(20)

GROUP SCORES

4	⊥⊥⊥⊥ / /	⊥⊥⊥⊥ ⊥⊥⊥⊥
3	/ /	/ /
2	⊤⊤⊤⊤	/ / /
1	/ /	
0	/ / / /	⊤⊤⊤⊤

SUMMARY

Pre-	50 (12/26)	50 (15/26)
Post-	60 (9/26)	70 (5/26)
Group	2.3 (9/26)	2.6 (8/26)

Symbols (first column) indicate possible ways student may have shifted or failed to shift during discussion in choice of solution: R-W, right to wrong; W-W, wrong to wrong; W-R, wrong to right; R-ns, right at start and made no shift; W-ns, wrong at start and made no shift. Number of tally marks opposite each symbol indicates number of times student experienced that kind of shift, or failed to shift. In the first twenty discussions, the record above shows that the student shifted from the right to a wrong solution once; four times from one wrong solution to another; four times from a wrong solution to the right one; eight times started with the right solution and held to it; three times started with a wrong solution and held to it. Horizontal bar at top of each tally mark indicates: if projecting to the left, student was in a minority (possibly of one) before discussion; if projecting to right, he was in a majority. Horizontal bar at bottom of a tally mark indicates that at close of discussion student was in a minority if projection is left, a majority if right. Bars show what actually happened during student's participation in discussion and suggest areas of improvement. Tally marks opposite group scores (4, 3, 2, 1, 0) indicate number of times student's groups achieved each of these scores during twenty discussions: 4 shows 80-100 percent of the members chose preferred solution at discussion's close; 3 indicates that 60-80 percent chose the preferred solution; and so on.

In preparation for the session on evaluation of performance the instructor has set down on each student's record sheet a summary of the student's achievement, indicating in round numbers the percentage of times he chose the preferred solution before and after discussion and his mean group score. After each entry he may also have indicated in parentheses a letter grade or, as in the Sample Student's Record Sheet, the rank in the class to which the score would entitle the student. At the evaluation session each student is handed his record sheet for examination. He can see at once how well he has done in comparison with other members of the class and, beginning with the second period of evaluation, how well he has done in comparison with his own previous record.

Suggestions for Improvement

In examining the data on his record sheet the student would do well to raise and try to answer the following questions:

1. How good was my prediscussion judgment
   a. In comparison with my previous record?
   b. In comparison with that of others in the class?
2. Could I improve my prediscussion judgment by
   a. Reading the problem and the solutions more carefully?
   b. Considering more carefully what the criteria should be?
3. How good was my postdiscussion judgment
   a. In comparison with my previous record?
   b. In comparison with that of others in the class?
4. How much did my judgment improve during discussion?
5. Could I profit more from discussion by
   a. Keeping the criteria more clearly in mind?
   b. Listening more carefully and open-mindedly to the arguments presented?
   c. Being more independent of majority influence?
6. How good is my mean group score
   a. In comparison with my previous record?
   b. In comparison with that of others in the class?
7. Could I help the group more by

a. More often being right in my own judgment by the end of the discussion?

b. Making more procedural suggestions regarding criteria and method generally?

c. Speaking up more frequently and persuasively in support of my own views?

In response to such questions the following comment might well be made in interpreting the data for the second period of evaluation from the sample record sheet shown previously:

Prediscussion judgment: The student's chief weakness is in his prediscussion judgment, as it was during the first twenty discussions. He still starts with the preferred solution only 50 percent of the time. As the class has improved somewhat in this respect, he now ranks fifteenth rather than twelfth in the class. During preliminary study of the problem he should read the problem and solutions more carefully, try to decide what the criteria ought to be, and keep these criteria in mind as he chooses a solution.

Postdiscussion judgment: Here the student has made substantial improvement and now ranks in the top fifth of the class. As during the first twenty discussions, he changes his mind freely during discussion, holding to a wrong solution only three times out of twenty, but he now changes his mind more judiciously than formerly. To profit even more from discussion, he should be still more judicious in changing his mind, keeping the criteria in view during discussion and weighing carefully the arguments on each solution.

Group score: In helping the group to make a wise decision he has improved substantially, but so has the rest of the class; so that he still ranks only in the upper third of the class. Since by the end of discussion he is right 70 percent of the time, he might help the group to a greater degree by speaking up more frequently and persuasively in defense of his own views.

Below are a number of the questions students often ask in attempting to interpret the data on their record sheets, and the answers an instructor is likely to make to each.

Q. What is the significance, if any, of a large number (six to eight out of twenty) of majority-to-minority shifts?

A. If, in most cases, you were shifting from a wrong solution to the preferred solution, you are doing well; you profit more from the discussion than the majority does and have the courage to abandon the majority when you find that they are wrong. If, however, in most cases you are shifting from a wrong solution to another wrong one or from the preferred solution to a wrong one, be more open-minded; the majority is more often right than you are. Keep the criteria in mind during discussion; listen to and weigh the arguments carefully and don't shift unless really convinced that you are wrong.

Q. What does it mean when I have made many minority-to-majority shifts?

A. Again it depends upon whether you are shifting to the preferred solution or to a wrong one. If you are shifting to the preferred solution, you are doing well; you are a judicious listener and profit from what you hear. But if in most cases you are moving to a wrong solution, you are too easily influenced by the majority. Keep the criteria in mind and weigh the arguments carefully, but don't go along with the majority just to be on the band wagon; the majority is often wrong.

Q. What does it mean when I make many minority-to-minority shifts?

A. Probably that you are not easily influenced by the majority. This is good if you are shifting to the preferred solution. If not, it means that you are not profiting from the discussion. Listen more open-mindedly, weigh the arguments very carefully, and don't make up your mind until near the end of the discussion.

Q. What does it mean when I make many majority-to-majority shifts?

A. Again it depends upon whether in most cases you are moving to the preferred solution. If you are, you are profiting from the discussion. If you are often moving to a wrong solution, it means that you are following the majority too blindly. Be more independent in your thinking.

Q. What should I do about many wrong-no shifts?

A. You are too inflexible. Listen more open-mindedly, weigh the arguments carefully, and be more willing to change your mind.

Q. What should I do about many wrong-to-wrong shifts?

A. If you are usually following the majority in these shifts, be more independent; the majority is often wrong. If you are not following the majority and still make many wrong-to-wrong shifts, you probably are not listening carefully. Keep the criteria in mind and weigh the arguments open-mindedly.

Q. What should I do about many right-to-wrong shifts?

A. This depends upon whether in these shifts you are following the majority. If you are, you are too easily influenced by the majority. Be more independent. If you are not following the majority, be more judicious and thoughtful during discussion. Keep the criteria in mind and don't shift unless by the end of the discussion you become convinced you are wrong.

Q. If one of my summary scores, say that on postdiscussion judgment, ranks me about 16/30 in the class, does this mean I have not improved?

A. Not necessarily. If 16/30 is about where you ranked in the class at the previous evaluation period, it means that you have improved about as much as the rest of the class. If your previous ranking was, say 25/30, you have improved more than the rest of the class; if your previous ranking was, say 5/30, you have improved less than the rest of the class, though you may still have improved some. The best check on whether you have improved is to compare your summary scores with your own previous record.

C. A Controversial
Radio Panel Discussion

The following discussion was broadcast over Station WOSU on December 7, 1962.

Question: Is capital punishment necessary?

Moderator: Dr. James Lynch

Panel: Professor Lawrence Herman, College of Law, The Ohio State University

Mr. Earl W. Allison, Prosecuting Attorney, Franklin County, Ohio

Lynch: This is the second of two programs on capital punishment. Last week we looked into the definition of capital punishment and considered its history here in the United States and in other parts of the world and its application in the state of Ohio. We discussed also what first degree murder is in the state of Ohio and under what circumstances a prosecuting attorney would call for capital punishment. Our two guests, Professor Lawrence Herman, of the Ohio State University College of Law, and Mr. Earl W. Allison, Prosecuting Attorney for Franklin County in the state of Ohio, are certainly on opposite sides of the fence. Mr. Allison fully supported the argument that capital punishment does work as a strong deterrent to capital crime. Mr. Herman, on the other hand, cited evidence to the contrary and disagreed with this basic argument. Well, let's move along now and consider other arguments for and against capital punishment. Or perhaps one or both of you gentlemen may want to add something to your comments about capital punishment as a deterrent to crime. Is there anything you want to add to what you said last week?

Herman: I'd like to add this to the comments I made concerning Professor Sellin's statistical study. Last week I indicated that his study involved a comparison of states having similar economic conditions and population components. The study was far broader than that. A second study sought to determine whether the police were safer in capital punishment states than they were in abolition states. The evidence that Professor Sellin found was again inconclusive. He could not say that in those states in which capital punishment has been abolished the policeman's life is a more hazardous one than in those states in which capital punishment has been retained. A third part of his study embraced those states in which there has been experimental abolition. In some states which started off with capital punishment, there was abolition of capital punishment, and then capital punishment was subsequently restored. If capital punishment does act as a deterrent, one would expect that during the period of abolition the homicide rate would increase and during the period of retention there would be a corresponding decrease. Again the statistics failed to bear this out. What the statistics demonstrated was that in those years in which there was an increase in the homicide rate there was a corresponding increase in rate throughout the United States. In those years in which there was a decrease in the homicide rate there was a corresponding decrease throughout the United States. Nothing in these figures gives us any basis for pinpointing the abolition or the restoration of capital punishment as a cause for fluctuation. Finally—and while the statistical base in this area, I think, is inadequate, the point is interesting and I believe it merits some comment— a minor study was attempted in Philadelphia to determine whether the imposition of the capital sentence or the execution of the capital sentence would have any effect on the homicide rate. A certain period of time was selected, say two weeks, before the sentence was imposed or executed and a corresponding period after the imposition or execution of the sentence. It was found that more capital crimes were committed after the imposition or execution of the capital sentence than before. There was no evidence to indicate that the imposition or the execution of the sentence had the effect of cutting down the crude homicide rate. Now admittedly this deals with just a few cases and just a short period before and after sentence or execution of sentence.

Lynch: Well, Mr. Allison, you pointed out last week, I think, that capital punishment was a deterrent to the commission of capital crime in the future, and one of your strong points was that there is an immeasurable effect on the potential capital offender of the future. We don't know how many crimes were *not* committed because of capital punishment. But if capital punishment were abolished, what would happen? What's the alternative?

Allison: Well, of course, to many people this is one of the strongest arguments for the retention of capital punishment, because no one has come up with a satisfactory alternative. The proposal has been made that we just substitute the life sentence. This would be fine in many cases, but—as we well know—life sentence does not mean life imprisonment in the state of Ohio. A person who is serving a life sentence is eligible at the end of twenty years for a commutation of his conviction to second-degree murder and then becomes eligible for parole. Many of these persons who are paroled, who have been guilty of first-degree murder, are deserving of parole. They do return to society. They do make good citizens. These are usually the type for whom the death penalty was not asked in the first place; their first-degree murders arose primarily out of domestic situations, or something of that nature. To me, however, in the case of other types of murders, eligibility for parole at the end of twenty years would be a highly unsatisfactory solution. Some persons propose even a more drastic change. They would like to substitute an indefinite sentence whereby the murderer might well be able to return to society in a matter of five years, for example. To me, this also is unsatisfactory.

Lynch: Who would determine whether they're ready to re-enter society?

Allison: I would presume that this would be determined by the Pardon and Parole Commission or by some new agency in the event of the abolition of capital punishment. Some new agency might be created by the legislature.

Lynch: Is there any evidence to support the idea that if a person is in prison and is rehabilitated or sent back to society he commits the same crime again? Do we have facts to back this up?

Herman: As I pointed out last week, the California study showed that about 10 percent of paroled capital felons, felons who had committed capital felony but who had not received the death penalty, returned to prison. Most of these were for parole violations but a few were for committing other offenses. Very, very few were for a capital offense. In terms of risk to society, the capital offender poses far less risk than does the forger, the automobile thief, or the burglar. Now I agree with Mr. Allison in his statement that a sentence to life imprisonment does not mean that the defendant will actually serve out his remaining years in a penal institution. And I think it should be that way. I think we ought to have ways whereby those who are far more trained in the science of the mind than lawyers and judges, for example, can express an opinion as to whether or not there is any risk in returning a particular individual to society.

Lynch: Do we always know? Isn't there a possibility of error here? Perhaps a psychiatrist could be wrong.

Allison: Certainly I think that psychiatrists, who are medical doctors, would be the first to agree that psychiatry, like medicine, is not an exact science. Certainly on any given individual, even during the trial of a case, we may have three psychiatrists on one side who say that the defendant is insane and three psychiatrists on the other who say that he is sane. In that field no psychiatrist and no group of psychiatrists can put their finger on a human being and say this man will, or this man will not, ever again commit a crime. That is just impossible.

Herman: I agree. There is no dispute between Mr. Allison and me on that point. Our medical knowledge—our psychiatric knowledge—is not advanced to the point, and may never advance to the point, where a psychiatrist can say with certainty that an individual will present no risk to society. I do believe that we ought to take advantage of psychiatric know-how available to us—we ought to give these specialists an opportunity to express their opinion regarding the probability of risk; and as the California study has shown, the probability of any capital offender committing a capital offense the second time is very low.

Allison: I agree on this. It is a very rare occasion where a person who has once been convicted of murder in the first degree commits another murder. This might be true in cases of a paid killer or in the case of a person who is mentally unstable. I did not say a person who is insane; I said a person who is mentally unstable. There is a distinction. If he were insane to start with he should not have been convicted. However, when we talk about risk to society I become a little bit irritated on this particular point because I have heard so many arguments about the sympathy to be extended to a killer. In any closing argument in which I ask for the death penalty I usually phrase one of my statements in these words: "I ask the jury to show the killer as much sympathy as he showed his victim." To me there is too much sympathy for the killers and not enough compassion for the family of the victim and the victim himself. To get back to what I started to say on the question of risk to society, if you weigh the life of a person who has taken the life of another human being—or more than one—against the risk to another individual even in the rare instances where it happens, to me the killer's life is not as valuable as the life of the innocent potential victim.

Herman: I would say this. Last week I made the comment that I thought Mr. Allison's argument was rooted in vengeance. I think that comment is equally valid this week. The reference to sympathy for the victim seems to me to be rooted completely and solely in a concept of vengeance. Those of us who oppose the imposition of capital punishment do not do so out of an excess of tender-heartedness for the defendant in the particular case. Similarly we blot out from consideration the particular act involved, in terms of its brutality, because emphasis upon the brutality of the act or emphasis upon the life lost or the pain inflicted upon the victim's family smacks of vengeance. I would agree that the question is not one of sympathy. I think it is one of humanity on one side—a moral argument that we have not touched upon and perhaps we ought not to—and the utilitarian aspect on the other, and we have been in that area primarily.

Lynch: Certainly there is a lot of pressure brought upon the jury and upon the prosecuting attorney by outside factors.

Allison: That is true, but I think Professor Herman did not hear one word which I inserted. I was not speaking primarily of the past victim but of the potential victim of a repeat murder. This is the life I am talking about.

Herman: To which I would say that I think, in terms of the available evidence, the risk is so slight that, as I said last week, capital punishment becomes a cure for which there is really no disease.

Allison: There is a slight risk, yes, but let me ask you how slight you would consider the risk if you were the potential next victim.

Herman: Oh, if I were the potential next victim I don't think there is any question that I would view a slight risk as a tremendous risk. I have been in the position of being a prosecuting witness in a criminal case in which a relative of mine was involved and could not himself be the prosecuting witness. When I participated in that particular case I was aroused,

I was irate, I was ready in this simple battery and assault case to vote the death penalty if the matter had been put up to me. This was purely and simply a question of vengeance on my part. I recognize the vengeance motive in my own case. I recognize it in the life of other human beings. My position is, however, that this is not an appropriate view for a state to take in its penal system.

Lynch: Certainly the commission of a crime as serious as this calls for serious action. Now Mr. Allison says he doesn't care how small is the percentage of people who recommit a crime. If there is an execution under capital punishment you are pretty sure that that person will not commit the crime again. Is that the point you are getting at?

Allison: Yes, that is correct. As I said last week, when a person has shown that he is capable of committing murder by already having done so, to me this does require a very, very close look. Now Mr. Herman can say I am vengeful. I do not consider my argument on capital punishment based on vengeance. These are things which one becomes acquainted with. I have personally viewed the scene and the victims of perhaps as many as a hundred and fifty murders committed right here in Franklin County and to me seeing those and trying to make available anything that might decrease the number of them committed is very important. As you may well know, we had another murder this week which set a new all-time high record for the city of Columbus. I might point out that Professor Herman will probably say—this is the whole basis of his argument—that the murder rate is going up. Let me point out that while it is a new all-time high rate in so far as numbers are concerned, it is not a new all-time rate per capita. The population of the city is growing and the per-capita rate is probably more valid to take as a basis for statistics than just the fact that we have had 34 criminal homicides in the city of Columbus and six in the rest of the county so far this year, making a total of 40.

Herman: Well, I think there is something to the point that every homicide that takes place is an example of nondeterrence, but I don't choose to rest on that argument. I noticed in Mr. Allison's statement that he is in favor of capital punishment if it *might* decrease the capital homicide rate and in that I find the word *might* significant. And I think this word *might* is the core of the argument. It is my position that unless it can be demonstrated that capital punishment *has* a utilitarian effect—not might have, but actually does have a utilitarian effect—I will oppose capital punishment.

Lynch: To use a good lawyer's term, are you placing the burden of proof on Mr. Allison?

Herman: That's exactly what I'm doing.

Lynch: Could he reverse the position and place the burden on you?

Herman: He might. My answer, however, would be this: The taking of a life is a serious matter—I think we all agree on this—whether the defendant has taken someone else's life or whether the state proposes to take the defendant's life. It being such a serious matter, I think it is incumbent upon those who are in favor of capital punishment to make out their case first.

Lynch: Mr. Allison?

Allison: The only thing I can say is that the deterrent effect is already proved in my mind. I cannot produce statistics, as I pointed out last week. People don't come around to me and say, "I would have killed had it not been for capital punishment." It is proved in my mind and I will continue to be a proponent of capital punishment until some proof is presented to me to the contrary.

Lynch: Well, we are at a standstill on this particular point.

Allison: I think we are.

Herman: Obviously, we are. One view is the introspective view of the deterrent, the view that says, "Well, it ought to have a deterrent effect. Logically it seems to me that it should have a deterrent effect," and the second view that says,

"Let's look at the available evidence to see whether we can show that it does or it does not have a deterrent effect." Depending upon which of those two approaches you take to the basic problem, the answer will fairly well follow.

Lynch: How about other arguments? Is this *the* argument for capital punishment or are there other arguments that you—

Allison: This is one of the basic ones. There are many others. For the benefit of the listeners I will name three or four of these arguments. This does not necessarily mean that I consider them to be valid arguments. One is the cost to the state of Ohio to feed a murderer. Assume that he is a young man, let's say in his early twenties, who goes in for a life sentence and remains in the penitentiary—and that has happened—for some forty or fifty years. The cost of keeping each prisoner has been established, and keeping a murderer for that length of time would cost the taxpayers perhaps as high as fifty, sixty, or seventy thousand dollars. This is one argument that is frequently advanced. Another argument, as I pointed out earlier, is that there is no suitable substitute. If life imprisonment in the state of Ohio meant life imprisonment, then I too would say, let us abolish capital punishment. However, there is an argument against this. Many penologists, particularly wardens of penal institutions, say point-blank that the electric chair or execution by some other method is far more humane than sentencing a man to the penitentiary for life without hope of ever again obtaining his freedom. The argument against this is that where there is life there is hope, but the penologists point out that to sentence a man to a life sentence without hope of a parole is killing his soul and that if you are going to kill his soul it is far more humane to also kill the body.

Lynch: Let's interrupt here a second and get Professor Herman's arguments on the other side, first on cost and then on the imprisonment factor.

Herman: As to the cost factor, I would question any factual data stating that it costs more to keep an individual for life in a penitentiary than it does to execute that individual.

I think the available evidence is to the contrary, but even if it weren't, this is a problem of prison administration. There are ways in which the prisoner can be made to pay his way while in prison. Too frequently we don't accept these ways. Not infrequently a state prohibits the importation of convict-made products from another state and because of state pressure—legislative pressure—we may actually set up a system in which factually Mr. Allison's argument is correct. Now on the question of whether it is more humanitarian to put the individual to death than it is to keep him in prison for life, I think here the wardens who make the argument are arrogating to themselves God-like functions. If you look at the individuals who have fought through various appellate courts for their lives, you see that the individual himself would rather be alive in a prison than dead, even though he may be in prison for a substantial portion of his life. I would oppose any rule by which a sentence of life meant life without hope of pardon or parole. Not because it is inhumane but because I think it makes more difficult the problem of prison administration. The individual who doesn't have any hope of pardon may be more difficult to take care of than the individual who proceeds on the assumption, as Mr. Allison mentioned, that "while there's life there's hope." While there is an opportunity for him to get out there is an incentive for him to be good.

Lynch: Isn't one of the strong arguments, or maybe the strongest argument, against capital punishment, that there might be a mistake and that there is no way to rectify a mistake if a man is executed? Say that some error has been made along the way in the conviction of the man or there is evidence that is later uncovered. What evidence do we have to support this?

Allison: I have heard several opponents of capital punishment say that cases have been uncovered where mistakes were made. I know of no case here in Ohio where anyone could *positively* show that a mistake was made. However, this possibility does not concern me as a prosecuting attorney for this reason: I have seen juries recommend mercy even where the evidence was so clear-cut that there could be no possibility of mistake. If there were the slightest possibility of a mistake, I know that no jury I have encountered would vote for the extreme penalty. It is only in a case literally where you have unmistakable eye-witnesses, plus a confession, plus absolute physical evidence, such as finding the gun on the person of the murderer and matching it up with the bullets, and so on— it is only in these cases that a jury will impose the extreme penalty. Let me point out that until early this year the last death penalty imposed by a jury in Franklin County was in 1948. Donald Rineboldt in the North Hague Avenue grocery murder was sentenced to the electric chair—he has an appeal coming before the Supreme Court at this time. I might add that Donald Rineboldt told investigators after his conviction that he already had his next murder planned—his next victim picked out—if he got away with the first one. However, the jury weighs all factors very carefully; it is for this reason that I am not fearful of a mistake being made.

Herman: Let me make two points: First, the fact that capital punishment declines in terms of its incidence in Franklin County is, in my opinion, an argument against capital punishment. As the use of capital punishment declines, so any conceivable deterrent effect that it might have also declines. As the threat of death gets remoter and remoter because people know that the sentence is not carried out, the deterrent effect, if any, gets slighter and slighter. Now a second point— I am not as sanguine as Mr. Allison is—about the merits, perhaps demerits, of the jury system. I think there are enough documented cases—there are several excellent books on this, by the way, in which are recounted stories of individuals who were wrongfully convicted—for us to make a good guess that individuals have been wrongfully convicted and sentenced to death. The two leading books are *Convicting the Innocent* by the late Professor Borchard of Yale University Law School, and *Not Guilty* by the late Appellate Judge Jerome Frank. In each of these books, each chapter—and there are many chapters in each book—is devoted to a particular case in which a defendant was found guilty of an offense and in subsequent investigation it was disclosed that the defendant was not guilty. In several of these cases the defendant was sentenced to death. In one of them, as he was being led to the gallows, the execution warrant was read to the public and it turned out that in place of the defendant's name on the execution warrant somebody had substituted the name of the jury foreman. The warrant, therefore, was technically defective and the execution was delayed. Subsequently someone else turned out to be the murderer and the defendant was ultimately freed. But he was seconds away from a wrongful death penalty

Lynch: I certainly would like to continue this—I wish we could— but we have presented two programs now and I think we have certainly uncovered strong arguments both for and against capital punishment. I only hope that this very fine discussion by Mr. Allison and Professor Herman will make you think more about the issue of capital punishment and make you look into the subject a little more closely. Thank you both for being with us.

D. An Informational Radio Panel Discussion

The following discussion was broadcast over Radio Station WOSU on June 21, 1963.

Question: How can we stimulate creative thinking?

Moderator: Dr. James Lynch

Panel: Professor Harold F. Harding, Department of Speech, The Ohio State University
Mr. Lewis E. Walkup, the Battelle Memorial Institute

Lynch: A few weeks ago we looked into the subject of creative thinking with the coauthor of a source book on creative thinking and a psychologist who is doing research in creativity. They agreed that the creative person is the backbone of any society. They defined him as the person who makes constructive changes, introduces new thoughts and forms in science, the arts, and in government and education. His kind is not plentiful in society, and there are reasons for this scarcity. First of all, it is difficult to spot the creative thinker and second, even if he can be located, he is not properly encouraged and developed. The climate for creative thinking is not what it should be, and finally, we just don't know enough about the whole area of creative thinking. Well, the reaction to our program was so encouraging in terms of letters and phone calls that we decided to take another look at the subject, this time in terms of how you, as a person, can stimulate more creative thinking in your work, in your school, and in your home. Professor Harold F. Harding, of The Ohio

State University, Department of Speech, is with us again. As you remember, he is coeditor of a source book on creative thinking published by Charles Scribner's Sons, and he currently serves as consultant at the Battelle Memorial Institute in Columbus. Dr. Harding has long been interested in creative thinking and has done much through his lectures and publications to encourage the study and analysis of creativity. Professor Harding also serves as Commander of the 83rd Infantry Division, U. S. Army Reserve, with the rank of Major General. Our other guest is Lewis E. Walkup, head of the Applied Physics Group, Department of Engineering Physics, at the Battelle Memorial Institute. Mr. Walkup has his degree in engineering from Washington University in St. Louis, where he also has done some graduate work. For twelve years he worked in the field of ammunitions and explosives. He joined the staff at Battelle in 1946. Since that time he has been deeply involved in research in the graphic arts generally and especially in the new and exciting process of xerography, the first major breakthrough in photography in the last hundred years. Mr. Walkup has his name, incidentally, on about eighty patents in the area of xerography. Well, first of all, I think we shall put the same question to you both that we posed on the last program. Just what is creativity? Dr. Harding, do you want to lead off?

Harding: I should like to offer a definition by the poet John Ciardi. He says creativity is the imaginatively gifted recombination of known elements into something new.

Lynch: What do you mean by creativity, Mr. Walkup?

Walkup: Well, I'd stress the same thing. But we don't really need to be very rigorous about a definition for our purpose today; I think we really all know what we mean by creativity. It is actually, as Professor Harding has said, making new and valuable combinations of known ideas and ingredients. They must be new or they aren't creative. They must be valuable or the definition is really without meaning.

Lynch: What examples could you give of creativity?

Walkup: Well, to mention a couple: Newton's law of gravity and Laser light. The new work on Laser light is certainly creative. Incidentally, my friends who know tell me that all of the facts necessary to create or invent Lasers were available in 1930 but nobody hit it until just recently. This process of xerography is a beautiful illustration of a creative act by one individual.

Lynch: Was it really a flash of genius, then?

Walkup: It was a flash certainly and yet it was a sought-for one. This particular inventor decided that there should be a better way to make copies of documents. He flew in the face of the large producers of photographic equipment at that time and said this ought to be a simple physical process. He then was able by thinking to devise such a process and to patent it.

Lynch: We mentioned in the last program that it is difficult to identify the creative person. Can you give a list of qualifications or a list of characteristics that could help to identify him? What kind of a person is he—this creative person?

Harding: He certainly doesn't come in the same shape and size all the time; and it is a great mistake to think of him as a genius. The hard-working man, the plugger, can also be a creative man, one who by persistence comes up with ideas. I think, Lew, you will agree that the engineers and scientists at Battelle differ widely in their attributes.

Walkup: Yes, I think this is true. However, I think that for a creative person it isn't too difficult to identify another creative person. He is essentially problem-oriented. He is interested in asking the question "Why?" He has to have a certain amount of knowledge about his field and this has to be a peculiar type of knowledge that he can manipulate in his mind. The creative act really requires the combining of knowledge in new and different ways; he has to retain it in such a form that he can actually combine it differently.

Lynch: Well, does it necessarily take a man with a high IQ to create?

Walkup: No. The evidence seems to indicate that people with IQ's under perhaps 100 are not particularly creative, but anyone with an IQ above that—which means about 50 percent of the population—can be just as creative as the extremely high IQ. IQ seems to measure an ability to take IQ tests or to reproduce knowledge more than it does to think creatively. The creative person probably is marked more by his orientation: he's terribly intrigued with unsolved problems; he likes to think about the unanswered questions more than about the answered ones. He has sort of a hobby interest in this area. It must be something more than a professional interest; he must actually *like* to seek solutions. He is problem-centered; he is question-answering, question-seeking. Finally, he must know a few of the rules of the game of creativity, which we may discuss later.

Harding: I have heard you use the phrase "playing around" several times, Lew. You almost make me think at times that creativity is a game. What do you mean by "playing around" with ideas?

Walkup: Surprisingly, it does seem to be a sort of game. It seems to involve playing around. Obviously, if you stay on the beaten paths, if you think the conventional thoughts, if you consider the ordinarily accepted laws of science, you do not arrive at anything different. It is only when you throw discretion to the wind and literally play around with the concepts in a particular field that you are likely to come up with something really creative.

Lynch: What do you suppose drives a person to be this way, to play around with experiments and try new things? Is he born with that or—

Walkup: Well, perhaps, but it is the interest in play, the curiosity that matters. I suspect that most creative people when very young were extremely curious about their surroundings in some field or other. While you may be driven to create because of a desire for new inventions, as Chester Carlson was, nevertheless back of this, I think, is the childlike interest in simply exploring a field without any thought of serious intent at all.

Lynch: Well, is a creative person as interested in the normal type of reward or compensation as all of us are—more pay, better houses, a better office, and so on? Are these his drives, his interests, when he creates?

Walkup: Probably not. Of course, he, like any human being, must have something to live on, so that he must of necessity be interested in the ordinary rewards to a certain extent, but that really can hardly motivate him to do the type of extra-curricular thinking that is required for creativity. He has to do this because of a personal interest in it. He does it because it is a hobby.

Harding: Is it possible for a man to force himself into creating ideas?

Walkup: Probably only in secondary ways. I doubt very much that one can sit down and force himself at any particular time to think creatively about a certain topic. However, if he understands himself at all, he can consciously set up a situation in which he will become interested in a particular field. The creative person has a wide interest span generally so that he can *trick* himself, if one can use the word, into being interested and hence developing this hobby interest in a particular area. He can consciously want to create in it.

Lynch: Well, Dr. Harding, you mentioned on the last program that one of the best ways to start a person off on the right creative track was to grab him early enough, that is, in the lower grades or even in the home before he gets to school. Now let's be honest. There are a lot of people who have gone through that process and are now in their 30's and 40's. Is all hope lost for them as creative thinkers? Do we just toss them out the window and work on the younger people, or is there a way to help them?

Harding: No, I think it is possible to revive their interest. Unfortunately in colleges and universities we cultivate critical thinking, and many creative thinkers are pushed aside in this process. It is possible to stimulate creativity; it is possible to train the thinker, and to retrain him. The most important thing is to create the proper environment. We very much need to give attention to this in college and university classrooms, and I certainly think that in research organizations it is a matter of vital concern. In fact, American business needs to have a new look at the need for good creative effort.

Lynch: What would you say would be the best way to promote this in a person who is already grown and has been thinking in other ways and now wants to change?

Walkup: Well, first of all perhaps we should say—this is making an analogy—that all of us have some public-speaking ability and this is a little bit like creativity. Every one of us has some ability in this direction and it can be improved or enhanced by training. I think it is the same way with creativity. We can actually improve it at any age. Perhaps we would be better at it generally if we started when we were fairly young, but we can greatly increase our present ability in this direction. As to your direct question though—"How would one go about developing this creativity?"—I think there are fairly definite rules for doing this. I think one would start out by identifying some area in which he would like to create—perhaps a new arrangement of his home or writing a new song. One would then decide it is important. He would tell himself that it is imperative that he do this creating. Then—and this is quite difficult—he would have to put himself in something of a leisurely frame of mind. Creating can't be done on the run. It must have a leisurely atmosphere.

Lynch: Does this mean just having enough time or getting in a mood?

Harding: By sitting in soft chairs?

Walkup: Pretty much getting in the mood—but no, it doesn't mean soft chairs. I think my most creative periods sometimes come when I have a headache and lose interest in the ordinary things of life—the duties I should be performing—and simply say I am going to take time to do a bit of creative thinking or attack a problem—one doesn't think of it as creative thinking—I am going to take the time to attack a problem that I have wanted to attack for so long. But after you get in a leisurely frame of mind, the thing to do is to toy with the problem, to think about all of its aspects. You should have available a great deal of white paper and some pencils and perhaps a slide rule, if it happens to involve mathematics at all. Then you should spend at least an hour but perhaps not more than three to four hours simply writing down and musing about everything that comes to mind regarding that particular problem. Then you will put it aside. After maybe two or three hours you will find yourself unproductive. You will put it aside and then come back to it later.

Lynch: Is this a form of daydreaming like what we did when we were young, when we went off into thought about what might happen if such and such happened?

Walkup: I suspect it is very similar and yet there is a distinct difference. This is problem-oriented. I think a great deal of daydreaming in the conventional sense is really an emotional experience; one simply senses the feeling of having a million dollars or something. In the creative case you would be saying, "Could I solve this problem by doing this, for example?" You might say, "Suppose I made this very small," or "Suppose I made this very large," or "Suppose I threw out all optics and started using fiber optics," or "Suppose I tried some other completely different approach to it."

Lynch: I am wondering if this creativity takes place more in the sciences than it does in the arts and in other areas, or can creativity come anywhere in your thinking?

Walkup: I suspect it can come almost any place. I think even housewives or people in walks of life in which one doesn't normally think creativity is being required can act very creatively. I think the fixing of a beautiful dinner, for example, might be a creative act.

Harding: In fact, anybody who says, "How can I improve this?" is making the creative approach. There are always better ways of doing things.

Lynch: You are separating the creative thinker from the ordinary thinker. How do you make that separation? Can you put one type of thinker there and the creative thinker over here?

Walkup: Well I certainly think you can put the problem-solver on one side and the creative thinker on another. Much thinking —much in science, in fact—is done by people who know the laws of science, who are quite familiar with the facts or who know where they can get them. They simply organize these facts to solve particular problems presented to them. This includes probably the great majority of scientific activities. It's only when these people find they can't solve a problem that they must do the creative type of thinking. In other words, if the problem doesn't seem to have an answer. For example, if you have an engineering job and you want to know how to build a road, there is plenty of data on that available; but if you want to build a road that will not wear at all or that will be considerably safer, you must perform a creative act. No one knows how to build such a road. Or if you want to construct a new space ship—probably most space ships can be built largely by textbook or handbook information. But if you want to build a space ship that can get off the ground with the use of very little energy—this has not been done yet— you probably must make a creative effort. Take very simple things: if you ask how to preserve strawberries, any housewife can tell you how to do it; but if you ask how to preserve the freshly picked taste in strawberries, no one knows how to do it; and if it is to be done it will be through creative thought.

Harding: As a kind of rule of thumb, Jim, I would say that the ordinary thinker is easily satisfied with solutions and takes whatever comes along. The creative thinker, on the other hand, is full of constructive discontent. He is looking for a better way even after he has a pretty good solution.

Lynch: He usually starts with a question?

Walkup: Yes, the whole thinking process starts with a question.

Lynch: I wonder why. Could it be done another way?

Harding: He asks, why doesn't it work, or why doesn't it work better? Why hasn't this been tried before?

Lynch: I think of this in terms of my own daughter and whether I should encourage or discourage her when she asks wild questions. Since I have talked to you, Dr. Harding, my decision has always been to answer her, somehow. I wonder if this is a good solution for parents of inquisitive children who want to know the answers? Should you try to answer their questions in any way you can?

Harding: I think this is one of the burdens of parenthood. Indeed, I would say that parents must try to answer any reasonable question from their children.

Walkup: Probably they will still look for other answers!

Lynch: Can a man be creative in a field other than his own? Or must he be creative in the area he knows well?

Walkup: Probably the knack or the ability to create is common to all fields, so that potentially an individual can be creative in many fields after he has become familiar with the necessary facts in those particular fields. However, much time is sometimes lost by people trying to create in fields about which they know nothing. This is useless because they don't have the bricks with which they are trying to build a house. They don't know the facts.

Lynch: You can't ask questions unless you have a certain body of knowledge on which to base them?

Walkup: That's right.

Harding: And even more important than facts, I think, is knowledge of principles. Principles are basic. After acquiring them the inquiring mind—the questioning mind—can make a real contribution. This is where creativity comes in.

Walkup: But the fact is that many people have been creative, many scientists have been creative, in widely divergent fields.

Lynch: We talk about the creative person as a sort of precious metal. You press a button and he becomes creative and you say, "Well, I couldn't be as creative as he is." Is he such a delicate creature? Must he be nurtured and cared for or is there a certain amount of creativity in everyone that just hasn't been tapped?

Walkup: A little bit of both. There is a great deal of creativity in many people that hasn't been tapped. On the other hand, the general climate in many niches in industry is not particularly friendly or permissive to creativity. The few creative people who break through have pretty tough hides and are willing to fight for the right to be creative in spite of environments that are sometimes not conducive.

Lynch: This climate is an interesting area to explore. You talk about the "right climate." Must we make a certain climate for a certain person or is it something more than that? What is this climate you talk about?

Harding: Well, there are a number of attributes of a good climate. One of them is a genuine interest in getting new ideas. Your boss certainly has to be willing to receive them. Next, he needs to provide the time, and try to understand the process of getting new ideas—it isn't an easy process; he should be willing to give them approval and recognition. New ideas do come along and he must not be completely negative— as so many persons in authority often become—this applies to parents, too, unfortunately. He ought to be open-minded. I think I would say that of all the attributes required for the climate of creativity, open-mindedness is the most important, and willingness to receive new ideas, and to nurture them; they are sometimes pretty tender at the beginning.

Lynch: You seem to indicate, both of you, that this climate is not what it should be and that there are a lot of creative people who are probably frustrated. Are they frustrated by this climate? Can they express themselves in a satisfying way?

Walkup: I think there are a great many frustrated people, and

I think they could be a great deal more creative than they are. I should like to add something to what Professor Harding has said. A great number who could be creative people, or potentially creative people, are seeking some type of approval. There is even some evidence that a substantial percentage of these people haven't received the sort of approval they sought in childhood and that many of them are still seeking something they can identify with.

Harding: You call this "covert approval." I have heard you use that phrase, Lew. What does it mean?

Walkup: It simply means that it has to be implied. It has to be implied rather than spoken because we can so sham spoken approval that it has to be given by implication, and it must be approval of the function, not just of the product. The research man who is creative wants to be liked, he wants to be accepted or valued because of this function he has in creating new things. Not simply that he can lay a golden egg once in a while; he needs approval for himself because of his creative activity.

Lynch: Do you think the automated age we are moving into is stifling this type of creative person? Is he falling into a mold along with the machines?

Harding: I don't think he needs to. There is a great fear of machines and automation and changing technology, but it seems to me there will always be room for, and a place for, the truly creative type.

Walkup: I should think that automation will even bring more need for creativity. We are going to have to find something for people to do who aren't feeding machines. In other words, automation will do two things: it will take away the need for so much drudgery—so much routine labor—and at the same time it will require much creativeness to put these people to work, or at least to provide things for them to do in their leisure time.

Lynch: This creative person—can you locate him in a certain area? Is he drawn to certain industries or certain fields of endeavor or is he found in all walks of life?

Walkup: He's probably everywhere, though you will generally find him in the background. He's not a self-promoter. He will probably be the unnoticed person in a group because he's thinking about how the light fixture works, or something of that sort, rather than about how to attract attention to himself. He usually is a retiring individual, but he could be found almost anywhere.

Harding: You can most easily identify him, I think, by the fact that he is always asking questions that are hard to answer. And in the classroom—in a class of thirty I like to think that there may be two or three genuinely creative persons. They're easy to spot. They are forever asking the teacher questions he finds difficult to answer.

Lynch: Do you think most creative people recognize themselves as creative thinkers or just accept the labels that other people put on them as creative thinkers? For instance, I don't know whether I am creative or not. I may be but I've never identified myself as a creative person.

Walkup: I suspect that a lot of creative people share this experience. I think that it is a general property of human beings. We don't realize what we are until we catch a glimpse by reflection from some form of mirror, some reward.

Harding: I don't suppose Thomas E. Edison thought of himself as a creative genius.

Walkup: Certainly not early in life—until he was told.

Lynch: How about you, Mr. Walkup? You are certainly creative in the work that you do. Do you recognize yourself as being creative or do you call it something else?

Walkup: Well, apparently from some of the outward signs I seem to have some tendency to creativeness. On the other hand, I didn't realize this until certain secondary things came out, like the number of patents I have been acquiring, or something of the sort. It took an external mirror to let me know that I had any of this ability.

Lynch: I am wondering what sort of advice you would give. People listening in now would certainly like to know who this creative person is and they will be looking for him—in their own children or in their own associates. And I think there is still some frustration on the individual's part as to how he can change his way of thinking, how he can become more creative. Are there steps to follow, or don't you like to label steps in this process? Does the process just happen? What step would a person take on his own to move toward more creative thinking?

Walkup: Well, I think we talked a few moments ago of simply trying some of the tricks of creativity. Think about some problems, some things—reasonably small things in your own environment—that you would like to have changed, things in which you would like some improvement, even if it's only a better potato peeler. Or you'd like to know how to thaw out frozen food better. Try to take these as little challenges to yourself. Write down what the question is, how you might do it, how it could be done differently. Try to think of all the ways in which it might be tackled, spend a little time talking about it to others, and you may find that something interesting and creative will come out of this. Now it won't seem terribly grand to you because it is your own child, and it won't seem particularly new. It may, however, be really a creative thought.

Lynch: I am wondering about another thing. We talk about creative thinking as something that is needed and that we haven't had. Why are we attaching so much significance to it now in this period of our history? Why do we suddenly have to turn to creative thinkers now?

Harding: Well, I would like to answer that question by saying that we are in a brains race with the Communist world. It's a race in which we are trying to get the best scientific ideas as soon as possible and to cultivate the people who can generate these ideas. We are a great deal more competitive in this respect now than we were a century ago when we were in an economic race with other countries.

Lynch: I don't like to cut it off here, Dr. Harding, but I do want to mention a couple of items before we leave. If you, the listener, wish to get more information about creativity or you want to learn more about the source of creative thinking, read the book coedited by Professor Harding: *A Resource Book for Creative Thinking*. There is also an article by Mr. Walkup called "Individual Creativity in Research." If you would like to have these, please feel free to write to WOSU Radio here in Columbus, Ohio, and we will try to see that you get them. Now I want to thank both of you, Dr. Harding and Mr. Walkup, for taking the time to talk to us about creativity.